THE

ROAD

BACK

Dorothy D. Thompson
Kim & hope you enjoy. DT.

Dorothy Davis Thompson

THE

ROAD

BACK

A Pacific POW's Liberation Story

Foreword by Charles W. Johnson

Texas Tech University Press

This book was set in Caslon and printed on acid-free recycled paper that meets the guidelines for permanence and durability of the Committee on Production Guidelines for Book longevity of the Council on Library Resources. (∞)

Design by Lisa Camp

Printed in the United States of America

Cover art detail from U.S. Air Force photograph, page 110

Library of Congress Cataloging-in-Publication Data
Thompson, Dorothy Davis.
    The road back : a Pacific POW's liberation story / Dorothy Davis Thompson.
        p. cm.
    ISBN 0-89672-362-3
    1. Thompson, Dorothy Davis. 2. World War, 1939-1945—Prisoners and prisons, Japanese. 3. World War, 1939-1945—Personal narratives, American. 4. Prisoners of war—Philippines—Biography. 5. World War, 1939-1945—Medical care—Philippines. 6. United States. Army—Biography. 7. United States—Armed Forces—Nurses—Biography. I. Title.
D805.P6T52 1996
  940.54'7252'092—dc20
  [B]   96-17062
                                                                 CIP

96 97 98 99 00 01 02 03 04 / 9 8 7 6 5 4 3 2 1

Texas Tech University Press
PO Box 41037
Lubbock, Texas 79409-1037 USA
800-832-4042

CONTENTS

Foreword

On December 7, 1941, the Japanese attacked United States naval, air, and ground installations at Pearl Harbor, following them swiftly with air raids on Clark Field in the Philippine Islands near Manila. In a matter of days, they had destroyed for months to come the only power that might have slowed their advance across what later became known as the Pacific Rim, but which the Japanese then called the Greater East Asia Co-Prosperity Sphere. Within six months, they had conquered more than a million square miles of land and ocean formerly dominated by the British, the Dutch, and—in the Philippine Islands—the Americans.

During all wars, when the forces of one nation advance quickly to take over territory formerly held by "the enemy," civilians as well as members of the armed forces are often caught up in the net of conflict. In this case, more than 500,000 civilians—Dutch, British, Australian, Chinese, and American, among others—joined some 150,000 military and naval personnel in captivity. They had been living, serving their governments, preaching, traveling, playing sports, or doing many kinds of business throughout that vast area. Now their nations were at war with the Japanese. The nature of their captivity would be affected by several complex factors.

Japan had been a signatory to the 1929 Geneva Convention on the treatment of prisoners, which was intended to ensure humane treatment of both military and civilian personnel. The Japanese Diet, however, had not ratified the Convention and shortly after the war began, their government made it clear that Japan would comply with the terms of the Convention *mutatis mutandis*. This phrase, "with necessary changes," left a legal loophole large enough to permit whatever kind of treatment the Japanese chose to impose.

Decently feeding, housing, and providing for the varied needs of hundreds of thousands of prisoners seemed frequently to be beyond the abilities or the inclination of the Japanese captors. There was, however, little consistency in the degree of severity or laxity. In some camps—or in the same camp at different times—discipline could be casual and treatment reasonably humane, but at times, it was harsh, cruel, and capricious in the extreme. As the war dragged on and supplies grew shorter, conditions naturally worsened.

Complicating the mix still further was the Japanese soldiers' contempt for anyone who surrendered, which made life especially hard for military POWs. The usual brutal discipline within the Japanese Army combined with a common distrust or dislike of Westerners meant that both civilian and military captives could expect beatings and other physical maltreatment, made worse by chronically short food rations.

The civilians held at Santo Tomas University camp/prison in Manila—Dorothy Davis and members of her family, among them—were under armed guard, but no provisions were made for their care. For the first months, they were entirely dependent for their food on former servants and Filipino friends. Medical supplies were almost nonexistent. As conditions stabilized, they were permitted to have gardens and were, in the main, responsible for their internal affairs. But Japanese authority was absolute. Internees were required to bow to their guards and to submit to searches at any time—to be discovered in possession of a radio elicited the death sentence. Civilians interned across the Pacific were frequently in much more dire circumstances. Ten thousand of the eighty thousand Dutch women and children who were interned by the Japanese in the Dutch East Indies died in captivity. Military prisoners, whose death rate approached thirty percent, fared worst of all.

Dorothy Davis Thompson's extraordinary memoir reminds us that for all the statistics, each captive was an individual, a person with a life before the war and for those who were both courageous and lucky, a life afterwards as well. Many, including her fiancé, did not survive. For those who did, when the war was over, there was the long process of physical and emotional recovery. This book provides a glimpse into one life. Multiplied by more than a half million, Davis Thompson's experience tells something of the cost of the war.

Charles W. Johnson
Director, Center for the Study of War and Society
The University of Tennessee, Knoxville

1 | The Road Back

Orders or not, I pulled off my helmet to catch a little of the breeze from the slow movement of the open truck as it dodged shell holes in what remained of the dusty road. I wiped my face against my shoulder, grimacing as the nurse's insignia scraped my cheek. Even though it was February, my uniform clung to me and perspiration ran down my face—drops were falling one by one from my hair. I wanted to let my hair dry out a little, but when I realized that we were traveling between two rows of 105 Howitzers that were being fired down range from us, I quickly replaced my helmet and refastened the strap under my chin.

This was a highly secret mission, and we nurses had been told no more than "what we needed to know." I had arrived in Leyte, Philippine Islands, the day before, February 6, 1945, to join the 49th General Hospital. Less than six hours later, when what was to be my unit was alerted for transport to an undisclosed destination, I knew in my heart where they were going. But I myself received no orders and jealously watched and listened to the others as they got ready for their early morning departure. I had been waiting for this moment for sixteen months, and now it seemed my dreams were shattered. I fretted and tossed about on my cot all night, feeling that morning would never come. As soon as there was a little light in the sky, I made my way to the latrine, where I was met by the chief nurse. She asked me if I could be ready to depart with the unit in fifteen minutes. I think if she had asked me if I could jump over the moon I would have said, "Of course." I hadn't unpacked a thing since my arrival, because I didn't know how long I would be in the staging area. Moreover, when I heard the rumors of an alert for "somewhere," I was sure that I knew where the unit would be headed and wanted to be ready just in case. The chief nurse told me that she had not said anything to me the night before because she was sure that I had guessed the destination and she did not want me talking to anyone about it. The orders for my transfer to the 49th General Hospital were covered by a message of explanation, so she knew that I had been released from the internment camp at Santo Tomas in Manila, where I had spent twenty-one months, and that my father and sister, Eva Grace Davis, were still interned there.

When we got to the air field, I was instructed to board the first plane with the doctors and administrative staff. This was my first airplane flight. I had no idea what to expect, but I was much too excited to be afraid. When I climbed into the plane, I was surprised that there were no passenger seats like those I had seen in pictures. We were instructed to find a seat in one of the hollowed out places on the benches on each side of the aircraft. We found seatbelts behind each seat, bolted to the hull of the plane. Our supplies and luggage were stacked on the floor between the seats and tied down. Finally, a box lunch was delivered for each passenger, and we took off. We were soon flying high over the mountains. It suddenly occurred to me that those puffs of smoke bursting below came from Japanese anti-aircraft guns. I felt my heart skip a beat or two, and my stomach began to churn when I realized that those puffs were being aimed at us. I decided to keep my mind on the cribbage game I was playing with one of the doctors. In the army, there are more hours of waiting than hours underway, so I always carried a small cribbage board in my pocket. Cribbage proved helpful in steadying the nerves, too; it helped me block out what seemed frightening.

THE ROAD BACK

We had been flying for about six hours when I felt a change in our speed and the sound of the engines, as well as a change in altitude. I looked out the window expecting to see some kind of landing field below us but could see only mountains. As we got closer, I saw an open field that was fairly flat, but did not resemble an air field. There were no lights, no control tower, and no planes on the ground. I wondered where we were—certainly not near Manila, where it was densely populated and where we should have had a view of Manila Bay from the sky. We had to be in the northern portion of the large island of Luzon, perhaps between Baguio and Cabanatuan. Even after we landed, nobody could or would tell us where we were.

It was very obvious that we were not expected and that no plans had been made for our arrival. Nonetheless, the staff and men of a small evacuation medical unit seemed happy to see us. Since I was just a tag-along second lieutenant, I had no idea what went on between the two commanding officers, but I did know that the "mess crew" (the cooks) cheerfully set to preparing a meal for us while another group began to erect a large tent to house the nurses that night. I could hear some mumbling among the group wondering why the other two planes had not arrived. We had been on the ground for more than an hour and still there was no sound of approaching planes. I wondered where the other nurses were. I remembered those puffs of smoke we had seen and found myself imagining a variety of scenarios, all of which made me very uneasy. While we waited, I decided to visit the patients. As this was a temporary field hospital, I found them on field cots in tents without flooring. Here, the patients waited to be evacuated as soon as planes could take them to a more permanent hospital farther from the front lines. I had hoped that the patients could tell me something about our location. They really did not know any names of the barrios or towns. But when I asked if they knew whether any POWs had been released, they had heard that Cabanatuan, the prison camp where I believed my fiancé Don to be, had been liberated. They did not know, however, where the POWs had been taken or how many were in the group.

It had been sixteen months since I had received any information from or about Don. It had been three and a half years since our last date. Yet as long as there was a chance he had survived, I could not help fantasizing a joyful reunion. And now, it seemed I had real reason to hope we might still be reunited. My locket with his picture in it hung from my neck with my dog tags. My questions about Don were far from answered, but I found some comfort in knowing that Cabanatuan had been liberated. There was no one to ask about Santo Tomas, where I had spent nearly two years and had left my father and sister sixteen months ago. Intuition told me that Santo Tomas was in the process of being liberated, or had already been freed, and that this was to be our mission. Yet whoever in our group may have had this information was in no position to tell, and I knew I could not ask.

I had been talking to the soldiers for about an hour before we heard the sound of an approaching plane. It was totally dark; the only lights were dim ones in our tents, powered by generator. I was relieved that one of the missing planes was approaching, but the soldiers showed alarm. They thought the plane was Japanese and was about to strafe the field. All those who could dived under their cots. Just as the plane was about to land, the pilot apparently realized that the lights he was approaching were from tents and not on the landing field, which had no lights. He made a hasty ascent, gunning the engines noisily, then came back for another try. After three attempts he managed to land without mishap.

The nurses, relieved to be on the ground, spilled out of the plane, talking a mile a minute about the reasons for their delay. While they were still in the mess hall, we heard the sound of another plane approaching. We looked on with relief while the pilot who'd narrowly missed our tents taxied his plane to the end of the field and used its landing lights to guide the incoming plane to a safe landing.

As soon as all the nurses had been served supper, we were guided to the tent that had been erected for us. We were surprised and a little frightened when we saw some soldiers digging trenches around the tent and setting up machine guns. One of the girls asked them why they were placing machine guns so close to our tent. One soldier remarked casually that we were only a quarter of a mile from the front lines. On that note, we made ourselves as comfortable as possible on our cots, fully clothed.

THE ROAD BACK

No one even attempted to go to sleep until we had heard all the wild tales the nurses in the last two planes had to tell. One pilot had thought that their destination was what had been known as Clark Air Force Base. True, it was the only real airport on the island of Luzon; however, it was still flying the Japanese flag. He didn't realize where he was until he could almost see the helmets of the enemy anti-aircraft gunners. Safe on the ground now, some of the thirty-five nurses he had carried on the C-47 were actually laughing about nearly losing their lunches when the pilot made a power ascent, fortunately escaping the anti-aircraft fire that followed them. I think even those who had been frightened beyond words were now finding the story funny.

Finally the tent was silent and most of the nurses asleep. We were ready for breakfast and final instructions at five a.m.; the trucks would depart at six. We were told that we would be going through enemy lines and no one was sure what we might encounter. We were given instructions about what to do if we came under enemy fire. C rations for the day were issued, and our canteens filled with water before we left. Our last instruction was to keep our helmets on and securely fastened.

I had listened with interest to the chatter the night before, but the group was closely knit, having worked together for almost a year, and I did not feel part of the conversation. They did not know why I suddenly joined the unit, and I was not free to say anything that might divulge our destination. I wanted to make friends, but the circumstances and conditions did not lend themselves to friendly conversation. It was impossible to hear over the noise of the trucks and the howitzers, so I had to be content with my own thoughts, memories, and anxieties. I found myself thinking about my family and how I had become involved in all this. Possibly, even under other conditions, I wouldn't have found considerable common ground with my companions. Although we all were trained in the same profession, our backgrounds were, for the most part, vastly different, surely as different as the perspectives we brought to our current situation.

I spent my childhood in Shanghai, China, where my grandfather, David Herbert Davis, had been a missionary. He died before I was born, but I had come to know something of him through letters he had written to the Missionary Board to report his progress in starting the mission in Shanghai. He had met my grandmother, Sarah Green Gardiner, in college while he prepared for the ministry at Alfred University in New York. After they graduated, they married and remained at Alfred University while he pursued a degree as a Baptist minister. Their daughter Susie was born a year later, and when she was four years old, my grandparents decided that their work should be in China as missionaries. During this period in history, 1860 to 1934, China was opening up to many religious denominations. The Chinese were thought of as "heathens," and China was fertile ground for missionaries. Over the years Grandmother and Grandfather Davis made many comments in their letters about the work they were doing to convert the "heathens."

On December 11, 1879, Grandfather Davis addressed the farewell missionary meeting at Alfred Centre, New York:

Could you, my hearers, occupy my position today, you would understand far better than I am able to describe it, the deep emotion of my heart at this hour. The influences of the occasion have almost entirely unfitted me for making any remarks whatever. We are for a few hours in Alfred; and when I recall the pleasant memories connected with this place, during my school life and again behold the faces of friends, and listen again to the familiar voices of College and Theological instructors, and then turn my mind to the prospect that is before us, my heart is made sad. It was here that I received the greater part of my education. It was here that my soul passed through a great conflict upon the question of preparing for the ministry. It was in Alfred University that I received many new and lasting impulses to work for Christ. It was here that the thought that life meant work, earnest work, was indelibly written upon my mind. The thought that I may never see these familiar friends, and hear the voices of these teachers again, is an occasion of sorrow. And again, to break the pleasant associations with my younger brethren in the ministry, to be deprived of personal communion and intercourse with them, parents and relatives, is truly a heavy cross. We have been passing through trials every day since we contemplated accepting the mission work in China. There are still other trials before us; but we accept it all, most willingly, joyously, believing.

My grandparents left the comforts of their home in New Jersey for China in 1879. They traveled by train to San Francisco, where they would board a ship for Japan, then take a smaller inter-island boat to Shanghai. Travel by train in 1879 was slow and uncomfortable. There were no Pullman sleeping cars. Overnight stops had to be arranged and delays expected. They left from Alfred Station in New York State on December 11 and arrived in San Francisco fifteen days later, having made twenty or more stops. Most of this time was spent riding coaches with no dining cars. They purchased snacks from vendors along the way during the stops in small towns. They were cold and miserable when they arrived in San Francisco. My grandfather wrote to the Missionary Board, "We had little time for seeing the city; nor were we disposed to do so, suffering as we were from severe colds. The little that we saw impressed us with the thought that we had in our youthful imagination built a far grander city in this land of gold than was in real existence."

On December 27, 1879, my grandparents and Susie sailed for Japan on the steamer *City of Tokyo*. Grandfather's description to the Mission Board of this trip left very little to the imagination:

> The first night, I went to the stern of the steamer to gaze once more toward the American shore; but, this time I did not linger, for the great swelling waves rolled the vessel so tremendously that I suddenly felt an unpleasant sensation in the region of my stomach; yes, I did, though it may seem unmanly to say it, and instead of seeing what I desired, I saw my last native dinner lying on deck in a confused and disgusting mass. Now I felt that this was a total surrender of all that bore the name and character of America. It was indeed a sacrifice I had hoped not to make; an unwilling one, I assure you, but it was unavoidable. Though we had received our table-tickets, I did not feel like making any great demands on the bill of fare; but with all my inner strength I kept casting up my accounts. . . . The first day we felt, as some writer has said, that we might die, and a few days after we were afraid we could not. The pen of an angel could not depict the depth of misery accompanying this disease. I agree with Mark Twain who, I think has said that there is nothing in the world that will take out, for the time being at least, self-conceit as will sea-sickness; and again when he says

that there is nothing that will make one so perfectly self-conceited as to have the stomach behave itself when others are sick at sea.

I could tell from their letters that living in China proved to be quite an adjustment. Life there was very different from in the United States. The language was difficult, but it had to be mastered before they could even get started building a mission. They spent many months studying. As soon as they were able to communicate with the Chinese in their native tongue, the little Davis family started making trips to many of the villages within a fifty-mile radius of Shanghai to study the needs of the people and learn more about the culture of this tremendous nation. My grandmother's letters to a dear friend in New Jersey described how they made their way about. There were no trains or roads between the villages, so they traveled by houseboat on the many creeks and rivers that honeycomb the land. The houseboats were crude junks about twenty feet long and propelled by a long oar on the stern. A "coolie" rowed endlessly. If the current was too strong for the oarsman, a rope was attached to the bow, and coolies walked along the path beside the creek pulling the boat. The coolies chanted as they walked. My grandmother would stay on the little vessel with Susie while Grandfather conducted his business in the small Chinese villages. Large groups of Chinese would gather around to watch the foreign devils. They were fascinated by Susie, with her fair skin and curly blond hair.

In 1883, three years after their arrival in China, one of the established missions gave up their compound just outside the Shanghai city limits, and my grandfather took it over. In a letter to his board he said, "It is a convenient and very good place. I am to pay 3,000 cash a month, the equivalent of about sixteen U.S. dollars a month. [One cash was worth less than one cent U.S. currency and is now obsolete.] It is rather high rent, but the best we could do. The Presbyterian mission wanted it, but I thought the place should belong to us."

My grandfather wrote about the difficulties encountered during the building of the new school for the mission. Progress was slow, delayed by weather and primitive conditions. The first building was to be for the girls' school.

Grandmother Davis was anxious to start a school for girls. It would be a boarding school. Girls in China were not educated and did not have much to look forward to except one pregnancy after another. They were expected to work in the fields, taking their small children with them. It was not unusual to see them working with one baby strapped to their back and toddlers working at their side. Infant mortality was extremely high. The lack of sanitation and the practice of using human excreta to fertilize the crops were responsible for spreading many diseases. Few babies survived the first year. A pregnant woman working in the field would pause briefly to deliver her baby, pick it up and strap it to her back, then resume her work. No wonder Grandmother worked so hard to teach the girls and provide them a haven.

The first nine little girls to come to the school were from very poor families, so the mission had promised to furnish them with everything until they were twenty years old. Then the mission had the right to give them in marriage if they wished to marry. The oldest girl was eleven. They were taught to help with the cooking, washing, and sewing as well as to read, write, and do basic arithmetic. None of them had ever attended a school before, so they all needed a great deal of instruction. They had lived in tiny one-room bamboo houses, covered with thatched roofs. The cracks were filled with mud rather than plaster, and most of the houses had mud floors. As many as twelve family members lived together in a house. The cooking was done outside, and there was no running water or sanitary facilities. The children were dirty and hungry, and either helped in the fields or begged in the streets. I don't remember ever hearing that the families were unwilling to allow girls to leave the home. Girls were not held in very high esteem and were often thought of as just one more mouth to feed.

Grandmother and Grandfather had a second child, Ted, in 1882, and twin boys in 1887. One of the twins was named Alfred, after the university. Alfred was to be my father. His twin brother died of whooping cough when they were ten months old. My father was sickly as a young child and Grandmother would take him to either the mountains of Japan or to Mochansan, a mountain resort in China, every summer to protect him from the debilitating heat of Shanghai.

Marjorie Anderson Davis, the author's mother, in 1923.

Susie, Ted, and Alfred were educated at home until the age of sixteen, when they were sent to the United States to complete their education. During her first year in the States, Susie died of a ruptured appendix. My grandmother was devastated, and when my father was ready to attend school in the States she went with him to be sure he was properly settled before she returned to China. My father spoke Chinese fluently and

Alfred Carpenter Davis, the author's father, in 1923.

wanted to return to China, not as a missionary, but to start a business of his own.

As was the custom with the Davis family, my father went to Alfred University, where he met Marjorie Anderson, my mother. They decided to be married as soon as my father had established himself in Shanghai as a manufacturer's representative for electrical wiring and electronic

Eva Davis, at two years and three months; Marjorie Anderson Davis; and Dorothy Davis, nine months, in front of the author's first home in Shanghai, China, in 1918.

devices. My father returned to China soon after his graduation to carve out his territory all along the China coast and in Manchuria, Korea, Indonesia, Sumatra, and Malaysia. By the next year, 1914, when Mother graduated, he was able to send for her. Two years after their marriage my sister Eva was born, and I followed eighteen months later, in 1917.

2 | Shanghai to Manhattan

A sudden silence jarred my thoughts, and memories of my family brought me back to my present journey. The soldiers had stopped firing the big guns when they realized that there were women in the trucks going by them. They paused long enough to wave and give us the traditional "V" for victory sign as they whistled as loudly as they could. For once, we appreciated the whistles. The whistles gave me a warm feeling, a sense of being protected, even though by this time I knew that we were not out of danger. I was no stranger to troubled times and had learned to accept them philosophically. Some of my earliest memories as I grew up in Shanghai were of fighting between the warlords. These hostilities would sometimes take place in some of the outlying portions of Shanghai, not far from our home. Families in affected areas would take refuge in the homes farther from the besieged parts of the city. The mission started by my grandfather was in an area most often affected, and during these times our home was opened to the missionaries who had continued in my grandfather's footsteps. Many of them were actually distant relatives.

China had experienced turbulent times for more than two thousand years. During the nineteenth century, the British, German, French, and Russians had exerted pressure to establish trade and to modernize China. In the early days of the twentieth century, the new Nationalist Party attempted to do away with the emperor and establish a republic. There was constant fighting between the warlords, who were trying to take over, and the Nationalists, who wanted to unify China. The new Chinese Communist Party became part of the struggle in 1921. Each group had its own agenda.

This constant turbulence kept China from progressing except in the large trade centers such as Shanghai, where American and European influence provided wealth and prosperity to a few Chinese who had been wealthy enough to get an education. The contrast between the few wealthy and the millions of poor was tremendous. I suppose I had simply accepted conditions as they existed in the Chinese villages. All I had to do was to look out my bedroom window and I could see, over the bamboo fence that surrounded our compound, one of these small villages—not one hundred yards behind our house. Although we lived very comfortably, I was aware of the misery surrounding us but had become immune to the sights. Perhaps that was the only way that I could handle it as a child.

One of my earliest memories, at the age of eight, had a profound influence on me. The city of Chapei on the outskirts of Shanghai was attacked, and it appeared that the whole city was on fire. It was so close that we could hear the sounds of gunfire, smell the burning wood, and almost read by the light of the fires. My parents were not at home. My father had been called to duty with the Shanghai Volunteer Corps to help protect the International Settlement, and my mother was working at the canteen to provide food and coffee for the men. They would be on duty until the safety of the city was assured. My Amah (Chinese nursemaid) took me on her lap as we watched from the third floor of our house. She tried to comfort me and told me not to worry. "Only Chinese dying young, missy," she said. I have never forgotten those words and, even at the age of eight, I wondered why my Amah thought it was all right for Chinese to die. Life was cheap in China. Babies died; the young died; and those who lived did so in poverty. Disease was prevalent—cholera, typhoid

The Davis home in Shanghai, 1925–1936.

fever, smallpox, leprosy, and trachoma caused blindness or other damage that maimed their victims for life.

I was eleven years old when my mother, sister, and I traveled to the States. My maternal grandmother, Iona Pier Anderson, had suffered a stroke, and Mother wanted to see her. The last time any of our relatives had seen us was in 1919 when my mother had taken my sister and me to the States for a short visit. I was too young to have any memories of that visit, so I was eager and excited about the trip in March of 1929. We traveled by ship to San Diego, where we visited old family friends who had lived in Shanghai. We were to be in Hollywood with friends for two weeks. School was still in session, and we had already missed almost a month during the voyage across the Pacific Ocean. Mother had promised my father that we would finish the school year so that we would be promoted to the next grade. I would be ready to go into junior high when we returned to Shanghai in the fall.

California was in the process of testing sixth graders. Practice tests were being given informally in the classroom to teach the students how to take the state tests. When the graded test papers were returned to

Carroll Ray Hutchins and Dorothea (Dora) Anderson about the time of their marriage in 1919.

the students the teacher asked if anyone had answered all the questions correctly. No one raised a hand. Then she asked if anyone had missed just one question. I timidly raised my hand and was embarrassed to see that I was the only one to do so. The teacher asked me to repeat the question I had missed. It was about the phrase "pedestrian lane." I had never heard of a special marked-off lane where people could cross a street without being arrested. In China nothing was barred from the streets. People pushed wheelbarrows, coolies pulled rickshaws, and buses, tram cars, and bicycles all shared the streets. California had recently passed a law against jaywalking, and the schools had been teaching children not to jaywalk, so the entire class burst out laughing. How could anyone miss such a simple question? I wanted desperately to be accepted, and their laughter stung. I was sure they thought I was stupid to miss such an obvious question, and was even too embarrassed to look at the teacher to see her reaction.

THE ROAD BACK

Just as I was becoming comfortable in my new setting, it was time to move on. Our next visit was to Philadelphia, where my mother's sister Dora and her husband, Carroll, an army officer in the Quartermaster Corps, lived. We had enjoyed a two-week visit with them on Corregidor Island in 1926, when they were stationed in the Philippines and my cousin, Marjorie, was just a toddler. The Amah had been in charge of Marjorie's care, but I had enjoyed amusing her and naturally was happy to see her again. Aunt Dora had been an army nurse in the Ambulance Corps with the British Expeditionary Unit from Presbyterian Hospital, New York, during World War I and had been stationed in France. I remembered our previous visit with them and wanted to hear more about her experiences in France and more about nursing. She told me about going to school in New York City at Presbyterian Hospital School of Nursing. As fascinating as Aunt Dora's stories were, I had no idea that I would one day follow in her footsteps.

I knew it would do me no good to protest, but I was really distressed when I heard that my sister and I were enrolled in school again, even though we would only be in Philadelphia for two weeks. When I found that I was ahead of the other children at my grade level, I felt better. I had never been ahead in any subject at SAS (Shanghai American School), so I began to think that there might be hope for me.

Our next stop was in Panama, New York, to visit my Aunt Augusta Anderson and my maternal grandparents, August and Iona Anderson. Panama was a very small farming community, and Aunt Augusta tried to prepare us for the small country school. Even so, it was difficult to fit in. Many of the children came to school shabbily dressed and did not have shoes to wear. Aunt Augusta had suggested that we wear our most informal clothes so we would not stick out like sore thumbs, but even our play clothes made us look different. We were teased and almost shunned. Their favorite taunt was to call us "Chinky Chinky Chinamen."

One rainy day I wore my raincoat to school. I hung it in the coat closet, but when I retrieved it after school, I found it had been ripped with a knife. My aunt assured me that all of this happened because the children had so little. The Depression had started, and no one had much money. I found all of this somewhat confusing. Although we were not wealthy by some standards, in Shanghai we lived well, as did most business foreigners. In China, the appearance of living well was imperative, tantamount to saving face, a principle grasped swiftly by every business foreigner who was to succeed. Even when the new leadership was established, costing my father the devastating loss of a contract to supply all electrical devices for a new mint that was to be built in China, very few people knew that our family was having financial problems. In actuality, it took years to recover. Things would still be tight in 1937 when I left Shanghai to enter school in the United States. Nevertheless, to the children of Panama, New York, in spring 1929, I suppose we did seem wealthy. How ironic it seemed that what was paramount to our acceptance in China now set us apart.

I was glad when school was out for the summer and I could roam the farm and follow my grandfather around as he cut hay and tended cows. I loved to ride on top of the hay that had been pitched onto the old horse-drawn wagon. My aunt had borrowed a pony from a neighboring farmer for me to ride while we were visiting. It was a wonderful summer, and I was very sad when I had to ride Twiney back to his home farm. It was time to make our trip back to Shanghai. I was looking forward to seeing my old friends again and happily anticipated getting back to a school where I felt comfortable and where I felt I belonged.

The excitement of getting ready for our journey back to China and the anticipation of the ocean voyage softened any reluctance to leave the happy, simple life I had enjoyed during our summer on the farm. My twelfth birthday was coming up, and my mother had promised to buy me a ukulele in Honolulu on our way home. I was fascinated with Hawaiian music and dreamed of being able to play the ukulele and sing as well as the Hawaiian hula girls. It never happened, but it was fun dreaming, and I did learn a few chords.

Junior high and high school at SAS were constantly interrupted by conflicts between various warring factions. Barbed-wire barriers would appear; the Shanghai Volunteers would be activated; British troops would take their positions around the city; and the United States 4th Marines would activate their defense positions. During these uprisings, the enrollment at SAS would increase. Missionary children from the remote areas of China would arrive with their families as refugees. The children who were ready to start high school usually remained as boarding students when their parents were able to return to their missions. We received an excellent education at SAS. The teachers were dedicated and well qualified. I was not at the top of my class by a long shot. I was much more interested in horseback riding, field hockey, basketball, and swimming than in working for better grades. I did have a good time, however. My favorite hobby was horseback riding. I rode all over the countryside for fun and in horse shows and cross-country paper hunts.

The paper hunt was a substitute for the traditional British fox hunt. Riding to the hounds was not possible in Shanghai. Even the very wealthy did not own large estates—every foot of countryside was farmed to feed China's huge population. Consequently, riders could not give chase haphazardly across the fields, which were tended by peasants, each family working a few narrow stretches of land with a furrow between each strip. The peasants lived in villages throughout the countryside and struggled to exist by selling their produce. The villages were governed by self-appointed warlords who took every opportunity to increase their own wealth.

Hence riders in the paper hunt were constrained to pursue a paper trail instead of hounds chasing a fox. The master of the hunt was responsible for laying the course and accompanied by Chinese mafoos, stable boys, who carried sacks of shredded newspaper and threw handfuls of small pieces every few yards to mark the trail. The course was always difficult, with many obstacles—ditches, creeks, and uneven ground. Sometimes the farmers would move the trail to keep the horses from trampling their crops. The master of the hunt was also responsible for negotiating with local lords to pay for all damages, but I believe the money seldom made its way into the hands of the farmers themselves. It was a shame, too; the settlements were probably more than they would have realized from selling their crops.

The hunts, occurring each Saturday afternoon, were major social events. A hundred riders, members of the Paper Hunt Club, and a similar number of spectators would gather to await the signal to start the hunt. Each rider would be properly attired in riding britches, black riding jacket, white stock (a wide band or cravat for the neck), and helmet. I don't believe

Dorothy Davis, age seventeen, in riding attire, holding the hunting helmet purchased from her school savings the day before the bank failed, 1934.

THE ROAD BACK

Dorothy Davis (center) and riding companions in 1936, crossing a high, narrow bridge over a countryside creek on a snowy day, a rarity around Shanghai even in winter.

anyone wears a stock anymore, but it was an integral part of the correct riding habit for the hunt. It had to be tied in the prescribed way and fastened with a tie pin. It took me many hours of practice to get it right.

It took me even longer to acquire all the required parts of the approved hunt clothes, particularly the helmet. My parents said the hunting helmet was too expensive and that they could not afford to buy it for me. Finally, I got permission to use my own savings. One of the local banks had made arrangements for students to open accounts through the school to encourage the habit of saving. I had saved enough to buy the helmet and to leave just a few dollars to keep my account open. The day after I bought the helmet, the bank failed. Customers lost everything above fifty Shanghai dollars (the equivalent of about twelve U.S. dollars). I had my cherished helmet and a little money safely under the protected limit.

As I neared graduation from high school, I started to talk about becoming a nurse, but my father would not listen. He had already decided that I should attend Alfred University, where he was convinced I might find a more appropriate direction for a Davis. When I saw a letter from the dean, Boothe C. Davis, who had been president even when Father was there, I was sure that I didn't want to go to his and mother's alma mater. Apparently my father had already written to President Davis. The dean had answered my father's letter, saying that he was delighted that I had chosen Alfred University, since both my father and my mother had been such good students. That did it! How could I live up to their reputation? The thought of following Aunt Dora's footsteps was appealing to me more and more, but first I had to graduate from high school.

I did more than just ride horses—I was active in Brownies and Girl Guides, which later became Girl Scouts. My ten years in the program had been a very good influence. Our leader, Carol Morris, was a wonderful person. I think every one of us matured and grew under her guidance. She expected a lot from us, but she was always there when we needed her. Soon after I "flew up" from Brownies, I decided I really wanted to be a patrol leader and kept asking Mrs. Morris when I could take on the coveted position. At the opening of each meeting, the patrol was inspected to be sure every girl conformed to the dress code—polished black shoes, black stockings, clean uniform, tie properly tied, hair neat, and one clean handkerchief in the pocket. One day I was caught without a handkerchief. I didn't forget it as I dressed for school, but I couldn't find one and didn't have time to call the Amah and ask her for one, so I stuffed a white sock in my pocket. I carefully folded it and hoped that no one would notice. After inspection Mrs. Morris called me aside to tell me that if I ever expected to be a patrol leader, I would have to stop being so scatterbrained. I never got caught without a handkerchief again. I did become a patrol leader and then a Brown Owl, the Brownie leader.

My senior year came to an end, and most of my friends were busy making their plans for college. I finally convinced my father to let me go to the Presbyterian Hospital School of Nursing, Columbia University, but one of the requirements was to be eighteen years old by September. I would not be eighteen until the end of October. Complicating matters further, my father said he could not afford to send me that year. I would have to travel by ship to New York and, although the tuition was very small in 1935, it was more than he could manage. My sister had left for New York in 1933 to attend the Katherine Gibbs Secretarial School, whose reputation for placing executive secretaries was well established.

She had graduated from "Katy Gibbs" and already had a good job with a law firm in New York City.

I took a part-time job as a chemistry lab assistant at SAS. The hours were short and the pay almost nonexistent, but the experience helped to strengthen my knowledge of chemistry, which would be a help in nursing school. I still had time to ride and to start making preparations to leave for the States.

Aunt Dora and Uncle Carroll were once again stationed in the Philippines, this time with the quartermaster corps in Manila. Marjorie, my cousin, was now thirteen years old. My aunt invited me to spend a month in Manila that summer. My parents agreed that this would be a good time for me to be away from home and to gain some maturity before going half a world away from home on my own. In a way, I found it more maturing than I expected.

The Philippines were still a commonwealth of the United States, and therefore under its jurisdiction and protection. I always thought that officers of the U.S. Army were supposed to be both officers and gentlemen, but soon realized my naiveté in thinking they would always behave as gentlemen. I had been well chaperoned when going to dances and other social functions in Shanghai and had not known the freedom now granted by my aunt and uncle. My uncle introduced me to many young lieutenants who loved to party and often imbibed more alcohol than they should. I didn't trust their driving and had to be firm on several occasions, demanding to be taken home. After looking forward to this kind of freedom, I was really quite content to return home after one month. Nonetheless, I felt more equipped for the world at large and much more ready to go out on my own.

I anticipated preparing for nursing school upon my return to Shanghai, but I failed the required physical examination. My doctor found that I was extremely anemic because of frequent bouts of amebic dysentery, and he would not let me leave home until the problem was corrected. I was treated with painful shots of Emetine, a drug no longer used for amebic dysentery, as well as with vitamins and iron. During my enforced break from school, I decided to enroll in a typing and shorthand class at a local business college. A friend who shared my passion for horses, Peggy

Arnold, joined me, making the experience a little less painful. By the time I finished the course I was very glad that I had chosen nursing and not a business career. I was bored and uninterested in typing and shorthand and, therefore, did not do very well. Shortly after graduation, my father's secretary became ill and he needed someone immediately to help him out. It was the end of the month, and he had to send his monthly reports to the manufacturers he represented.

The *China Clipper*, which came through twice a month with the mail, was due to leave the next day. The *China Clipper* was a large amphibious plane capable of carrying large amounts of mail and cargo, as well as twelve passengers. The passenger accommodations were luxurious, with sleeping bunks and a dining room where gourmet meals were served by a steward at a beautifully appointed table.

An astonishing improvement over mail delivery by sea and land, which took well over a month, the *Clipper* made its trip from Shanghai to San Francisco in a remarkable five days. My father's mail could not wait two more weeks, or possibly another month, so despite my misgivings I went to his office to type his letters. By the time I got through, both my dad and I had decided that this was not my place in the sun. I was very happy to be relieved of my duties as secretary. I disliked sitting at a desk all day and had always had a problem with spelling. I really wanted to work with people, not files and reports.

By this time, my health had improved and my passage to New York was booked at long last. To be accepted as a nursing student, I had to pass an entrance exam and a personal interview with the dean of nursing and the teaching staff. Consequently, I had to arrive in New York City in the spring, even though classes would not begin until September.

Finally, in May 1937, it came time for me to sail for New York. My trunks were packed and arrangements made to have them transported to the freighter *Anna Maersk*. Because I would be on board the ship for six weeks, my wardrobe trunk would be placed in the cabin. The ship was anchored in the middle of the Whangpoo River, about thirty minutes upstream, because there were no docks to which oceangoing ships could tie up. We boarded the tender at the jetty on the Bund, the riverfront avenue with the Shanghai skyline behind it. As we made our way to the

The Anna Maersk, *the freighter on which Dorothy Davis sailed from Shanghai to New York City in May 1937.*

ship, I watched the skyline disappear, not knowing I wouldn't see it again until 1983.

Final goodbyes over, the realization that I was really leaving home left me with a hollow place in my heart. I waved to my mother and dad for as long as I could see the launch making its way back to the Bund. The ship's whistles gave several blasts to warn the sampans, junks, barges, and other river traffic that it would soon be on its way and they better stay out of the way. I was alone as I stood at the railing watching all the activity, hoping that I wouldn't start crying.

I soon settled into the routine of the ship. There were only twelve passengers on board, most of them considerably older than I, but I found my way to the bridge, where the captain and first officers were very friendly. When I expressed an interest, they allowed me to join the young Danish apprentice in his navigation lessons. We each kept a chart on which we carefully entered the ship's daily progress. We learned to use the sextant and calculate our positions by using mathematical equations, logarithms, and deviation of the compass charts. We would never have believed anyone who told us that someday computers and other automatic devices would take over all of these functions, or that one day no one would stand at the helm to guide the ship while in the open sea.

They even allowed me to take a turn at the helm. I often spent four hours a day at the helm keeping the ship on the course ordered by the captain. The captain and other officers could tell how accurate the helmsman was by watching the wake of the ship. I fancied that I was able to keep the ship on an even course as well as, or better than, the more experienced helmsmen.

After crossing the Pacific Ocean, we made our way south along the western coast of Mexico, where we saw many giant sea turtles swimming close to the ship. The captain announced that we would spend a day or two fishing for one. The ship would maintain its speed, deviating only slightly from our course in order to bring the ship along side one of the turtles. The sailors rigged the ship's loading booms so that a cargo net could be lowered to scoop a turtle into it, then bring it up to the deck. Many attempts were made before the net caught a turtle at just the right moment and it was raised triumphantly to the deck. As soon as we each had the opportunity to photograph the turtle, the chef hurried away with it, and the next day we were served turtle soup.

Our ship continued south along the west coast of Mexico, Central America, and Costa Rica, then entered the Panama Canal. This was my first trip through the canal, and I watched every minute as a man in a small boat rowed out to us as our ship neared the first lock. When we were close enough, a sailor from our ship tossed a rope toward the little rowboat. The man deftly caught the rope, which was fastened to a cable on our ship. This was the cable that would be attached to the "mule," a powerful engine that would pull the ship through the locks. As we made our way through the locks, I thought about all the men who had perished from malaria and all the hardships encountered during the years of hard, back-breaking work it took to build the canal. The water was brown and cloudy from the heavy silt. Once we had gone through all the locks on the Pacific side we went through a large lake and could see the heavy tropical flora all about us with very little evidence of any human inhabitants.

Six weeks after leaving Shanghai, we sailed past the Statue of Liberty and docked in Manhattan, where I was met by my sister Eva. I had to go through customs by myself, and the inspector went through every bit of my luggage. I had no idea what to expect because my parents had always taken care of this part of landing procedures. I was afraid that they would charge an import duty on the few Chinese things I had, the most important being a set of eight porcelain horses. These were small models of Mongolian ponies, each in a different pose. They were not expensive, but I was very fond of them. The inspector pulled each horse out and examined it carefully. He asked many questions about their origin, history, and value. I got carried away with the stories about their origin, how they commemorated the eight chargers of Mu Wang, the fifth ruler of the Chou dynasty, who ruled from 1001 to 746 B.C. I told him how attached the emperor was to his team and how he journeyed behind them throughout his realm in a chariot driven by his henchman Tsao Fu. I explained that one of the horses is always shown rolling on his back to symbolize his liberation from harness, and how the sets, regardless of whether they are produced in porcelain, crystal, jade, ivory, embroidery, or painting, must always be complete to have value in the eyes of the Chinese. Finally the inspector smiled and let me close my trunks and be on my way without charging me anything.

My sister was still waiting for me and, after making arrangements to have my baggage sent to Webster House, the business women's hotel where she lived, we took the subway to Thirty-fourth Street and Fifth Ave. This was my first ride on a subway, and I was thoroughly confused by all the noise of the crowds and the number of trains rushing up to the station. I wondered how anyone knew which train to take. They were all going to different places, the Bronx, Brooklyn, or perhaps Long Island or Queens. When the train stopped at the Thirty-fourth Street exit, we got off, and Eva guided me up the stairs to the street and daylight. We walked the short distance to Webster House on Thirty-fourth. It was called a hotel but was more like a boardinghouse for young business ladies. While most boardinghouses were converted from large homes, the Webster House had been a real hotel. The nine-floor residence was popular because it afforded girls not only the privacy of very small rooms of their own but also the camaraderie of fellow young women in the workplace. Meals were served in a pleasant dinning room, and there were parlors where friends could be entertained, as well as a pantry with a hot plate and refrigerator. Even in those days security was necessary in New York City, and security was good at the Webster House. The front door was always locked and could not be opened from the street. Guests and residents alike had to ring a bell for the doorman.

That evening for supper, Eva took me to the dining room and I met some of her friends. I embarrassed Eva by asking the waitress how the potatoes were prepared. She couldn't believe that I didn't know and very matter-of-factly said, "Why, they are just 'berld.'" When I continued to ask just what was being served, my sister gave me a sharp kick under the table. It was all the other ladies could do to keep from laughing. When the waitress left, I was given a lecture on the various accents I would hear in New York City. I also learned what boiled potatoes were.

There was a great deal for me to learn about New York City, and I had to learn quickly. Eva would be off to work on Monday morning, and I would be on my own. Much to my relief, she did take me to the Presbyterian Hospital on 168th Street, for my first appointment, just to be sure I got on the correct train and got off at the correct station.

My first visit to the hospital left me in awe. I was ushered into the Nursing Service office, where I met Helen Young. Miss Young was a legend at the Presbyterian Hospital School of Nursing, and her word was law. Miss Young's uniform was always snow white and stiffly starched; her shoes without a blemish; and her nursing cap perched at the exactly correct angle on her white hair, which was piled on top of her head and held fast with combs and the required hair net. The entire teaching and dormitory staff met Miss Young's dress code, and it was made quite clear to me that the students would adhere to the same standards. Miss Young told me that if I were accepted as a student I would attend morning prayers at 6 AM and would be inspected as we marched out of Maxwell Hall to go on duty. I would be required to keep my hair off the collar; my uniform must always be clean and pressed and my shoes polished. Students were sent back to their rooms to correct any infractions of the dress code, and any time lost had to be made up after hours. Memories

THE ROAD BACK

of earlier inspections when I was in Brownies and Girl Guides made me smile. Miss Young explained also that nursing students, whether in uniform or in civilian clothes, must always be properly attired. This meant that students could not leave Maxwell Hall without hat and gloves.

Miss Young believed that it was important for young ladies entering the field to change the commonly held image of nurses as servants who performed menial chores associated with bedside care. We were to be educated at the university level and able to make nursing decisions based on our knowledge of medicine, pharmacology, anatomy, and physiology. Our class was the first class at Presbyterian Hospital to be associated with Columbia University.

Once I had taken and passed the entrance exam, I was invited to lunch with the instructors to pass scrutiny. I sat as straight as I could and paid excruciating attention to my manners. Mostly, I took great pains not to be a chatterbox, an offense that had caused my father to excuse me from the table many times. Much to my relief, I was at last instructed to proceed to Brook's Outfitting Co. Inc., on Fourth Avenue, to be measured for my uniforms. The order was to be delivered to Maxwell Hall, to await my arrival in September. Collars, collar buttons, and apron studs would be furnished at that time. We were also given a list of required equipment. This included hair nets, tailored black oxfords with soft rubber heels, black cotton or lisle stockings, two fountain pens, a wristwatch with second hand, one pair of sneakers without heels, bathing caps, regulation school swimming suit to be purchased on arrival (cost $1.50), tailored white cotton slips, laundry bag marked with name, shoe bag, and one trunk for storage.

Tempering my euphoria was a solemn caveat about the six-month probationary period. During this period, we would be required to wear a drab gray uniform with an apron—no bib or cap. Any infraction of the rules or failure to pass a course would result in dismissal from the school. If we survived this difficult period, we would be measured again for the coveted blue-and-white pinstriped uniform and would be "capped" in a very solemn candle-lit service.

I was very happy to have been accepted at the difficult and prestigious school and wished I could begin right away, but the whole summer was ahead of me, and I had very little money. I wasn't sure what my parents expected me to do, but I decided to look for a job. I saw some ads in the paper for camp counselors. Hoping I could get a job as a riding instructor, or at least an assistant, I set off alone for some interviews.

With Eva's help I managed to find my way around and landed a job during my first interview at a YWCA camp up the Hudson River in the Bear Mountain area. They had already hired a riding instructor, but my acceptance to nursing school convinced them to hire me as the camp nurse's assistant. I wasn't sure what they would expect me to do, but it sounded good. In the very least, it promised me a place to stay for the summer as well as good food. I don't remember whether there was any salary; if there was, it was very little. I already had all the proper clothes for camp and happily packed my things for the trip up the Hudson River. I was assigned to one of the huts with about six teenage campers. I met the nurse and found that my duties would not be very arduous, and I would have time to help with the swimming, crafts, and riding.

On the second day of camp, the riding instructor was bitten on the thigh by a horse. She was incapacitated for quite a while, and I was more than happy to take over her duties. I enjoyed the outdoors and everything about the camp. It was a very good experience for me and helped a great deal to get me ready for the three years of hard work ahead.

One day, in early September, a few days before summer camp ended, the daily paper arrived with the three-inch-tall heading "Shanghai, China bombed by Japanese—City under siege." I was so upset that I ran off by my myself and cried until I was ashamed to return to the camp. When I got back, I found that the leaders had been concerned about my absence. I had missed having my picture taken with the other counselors. This was a traditional picture for the record of each summer camp and marked the end of the season.

I told them I couldn't shake my anxiety and fear for my parents' safety. I called my sister. Eva agreed to come up to the camp and spend the weekend with me so we could work things out as best we could. This helped—having a chance to voice my fears enabled me to pull myself together enough to finish out the summer and return to New York. As it turned out, Shanghai was blockaded by the Japanese. No one would be

Eva Davis, right, visiting her sister Dorothy, left, at YWCA camp on the Hudson River in September 1937, the weekend after the sisters learned that the Japanese had bombed Shanghai.

able to leave or get any mail out for six months, and, indeed, my meager funds would be cut off.

Back in New York, I threw myself into getting ready for school so I didn't have time to dwell on my predicament. My father, through various Chinese connections, managed to have a cable sent from Hong Kong saying they were safe. It was time to devote all my energy to coping with another way of life.

3 | Career in the Making

I looked forward to starting my new career and wondered where it would lead me. In school we had read about some of the pioneers in nursing—Florence Nightingale and Clara Barton, who had been motivated by the terrible battlefield conditions during the wars of their time and place. I was motivated by the stories my aunt had told about her experiences in France during World War I, and by the suffering I had seen in China.

It was with growing excitement and anticipation that I reported to Columbia University—Presbyterian Hospital School of Nursing, on the banks of the Hudson River, just one mile from the George Washington Bridge. Seventy-nine young and eager students from near and far were enrolled in the September 1937 section. Some students arrived by automobile accompanied by their parents. The drive from New Jersey via the George Washington Bridge did not take long, but most students arrived by train or bus from their homes in Connecticut, Pennsylvania, upper New York State, or farther. I found myself drawn to two other students whose homes were far away, Marietta Papasaphiropouou (shortened to Papasaph) and Katie Saliari from Greece. They had been sent to Columbia University—Presbyterian Hospital School of Nursing by the Near East Foundation and were to return, upon graduation, to teach in the nursing school at Athens. They both spoke English well and were very good students. We all hurried to get unpacked and to settle in our little dormitory rooms. Most of the rooms accommodated one student and looked very much like my sister's room at Webster House. I was very happy with my room since it faced the Hudson River and had a wonderful view of the Palisades and the George Washington Bridge. Our new uniforms were waiting for us and we eagerly tried them on to be sure they fit; then we attended an orientation, where we learned more about the rules and regulations we were expected to follow.

As probationers, we stood out like sore thumbs, and I think that most of us felt very vulnerable. We were instructed to stand with our hands behind our backs whenever speaking to a physician, upperclassman, instructor, or graduate nurse. This meant that we spent a great deal of time in that position. I still find myself assuming this position when talking to people in high positions. Our uniforms left no doubt in anyone's minds as to where we were in the pecking order. Our class schedule was heavy with a great deal of outside work to be done—studying, writing papers, preparing for tests, learning practical skills,and taking care of patients—so there was very little time for recreation. My idea of living it up was to walk to the corner drugstore with a group of student nurses for a toasted cheese sandwich and a chocolate malted milk. We had a swimming pool in the dormitory basement, and I tried to find time each evening to swim twenty lengths before going to bed. The biggest problem I had with that was finding someone to go to the pool with me. It was against rules to swim alone. I never did find anyone to swim with me, but I could usually find someone to sit by and study while I swam.

We attended anatomy and physiology with the first-year medical students. These classes were held in one of the physicians' and surgeons' classrooms in Sturges Hall of the medical school. The seats were in steep tiers around the center amphitheater and had foldup seats. Some of the nursing students were so busy looking around at the medical students that they had difficulty paying attention to the lecturer. One girl fell into

THE ROAD BACK

the lower level of seats because she was trying to get the attention of a good-looking young medical student. She wasn't hurt, but she certainly got the attention of more than one student, not to mention the professor.

Once we had completed some of the basic courses—essentials of nursing, followed by many specialized areas of nursing—we started attending classes in bedside nursing. We had a practice classroom in the dormitory that had been set up with several beds and all the other hospital equipment that we would find on the hospital units when we started our actual bedside nursing. Each of us had to take a turn at being the patient so that we would know what it was like to be subjected to the procedures.

Seventy-nine had started in our class, but at the end of six months, when we were getting ready to shed our probation uniforms, change into the coveted blue-and-white striped uniform, and proudly receive our caps, there were only fifty-six students. We were very proud of our caps and, until 1983, when I retired, I wore mine with pride. We still had to wear the hated black shoes and stockings so that no one would mistake us for graduate nurses.

Although we had passed the first step and were now on our way to making it to graduation day, we still had a very busy schedule. Daily classes continued, and our hours and responsibilities on the wards grew steadily. During the first year we spent our practicum sessions in the general medicine and surgical units. Specialty services would come later. For some special services we would spend three months at a time at hospitals such as the Eye Institute, Institute of Neurology, and the Psychiatric Institute, all connected to Presbyterian Hospital Medical Center, but in separate buildings. For some services students would be sent to the city Communicable Disease Hospital, of the New York City Public Nursing Department. Nursing students from other well-known large hospitals in New York, such as Bellevue and others, would join us for some of the specialties offered at Presbyterian. Babies Hospital, in another building within the medical center, was well known for the continuing advances in infant and child care, as was Sloan Hospital for maternal care. We would spend three months in the operating room, where we learned a great deal about the importance of sterile technique. Antibiotics were just being discovered and infection was a primary killer.

That first year in general medicine, most of our patients were hospitalized for pneumonia. We were told that just one year earlier about 50 percent of the patients with pneumonia died, but since they had begun administering prontosil or sulfapyridine, the death rate had dropped significantly. These drugs had more side effects than the newer and more sophisticated drugs now given, as I found out when I developed a streptococcic sore throat followed by rheumatic fever.

I was working on a surgical unit and had been given the assignment of dressing nurse. I loved preparing the instruments and equipment for the dressing changes during grand rounds. These rounds were held daily when the chief of service held forth with the chief resident,. interns, and medical students on the service. Everything had to be prepared the previous evening before the dressing nurse went off duty so that there would be no delay when the 7 AM rounds began. The dressing nurse was also responsible for preparing the IV tubing and sets, and the hypodermoclysis tubing and sets. Reusable latex tubing was used and had to be very carefully cleaned and then rinsed with distilled water before sterilization. The tubing used for blood transfusions was particularly difficult to clean. All the needles were cleaned, sharpened, and sterilized in the work room as well. I was very impressed with my responsibility and thought the world would probably come to an end if I didn't show up in the morning for rounds, so when my throat started to hurt that afternoon, I ignored it.

Fortunately, one of my friends could tell I was not feeling well and that my throat hurt. She told me that I should report to the nurse in the infirmary. I went to bed, hoping I would feel better in the morning. At about nine in the evening I was called by the nurse at the student dormitory infirmary and instructed to report there immediately. When I got there I had a fever and my red throat was cultured; furthermore, I was ordered to bed in the infirmary. When I got up in the morning, I found that my ankles were swollen, red, and painful—so painful that I had to limp to the bathroom, where I was caught by the nurse on duty, who ordered me back to bed and called the infirmary doctor to see me. A sedimentation rate was ordered and found to be elevated. The culture for beta-hemolytic streptococcus was positive. I was put on prontosil and large doses of aspirin. The aspirin reduced the swelling and redness in my ankles. I was put on bed rest for two weeks, then told I would have to take a thirty-day convalescent period at home.

Well, of course, I couldn't go home. Even if I could have made it to and from China in a month, I would not have been permitted to enter Shanghai since the Japanese had taken over the city. My parents had told me that Henry Gregory, an old-time friend, who had been with the British-American Tobacco Company, had agreed to keep an eye on me while I was in school. He now lived in Rocky Mount, North Carolina, with his wife, Hattie. Jane, their only child, was at Duke University Medical School. My sister and I had known her since early high school years. My sister was one year ahead of Jane and I was one year behind, but the three of us had been very active in scouting, and Jane occasionally rode horseback with my group. Jane and Eva had left Shanghai together and enjoyed a wonderful trip on the *Empress of Canada*, as well as on the train trip from Vancouver to New York City. Before medical school, Jane had graduated from Bryn Mawr in Pennsylvania. I think she was in her second or third year at Duke University. With considerable apprehension I called the Gregorys and told them of my problem. They promptly invited me to come to Rocky Mount and to stay as long as I needed.

I left the next day by train. The train ride took about eight hours. The coach was uncomfortable: no modern reclining seats and no air conditioning. The open windows let in the soot that blew in from the engines, and I was soon covered with it. The train did not pull into the Rocky Mount station until almost midnight. I think I was the only person getting off the train so it was not hard for Nathan, the Gregory's chauffeur, to find me. He took my bag and helped me into the car, explaining that since it was so late, the Gregorys had retired and he would show me my room so I could get to bed as quickly as possible. I was grateful that I would have the opportunity to get cleaned up and get some rest before seeing them. I was exhausted. My room was very comfortable, with an adjoining bath, so I quickly washed the soot off my face and hands and fell into bed.

When I got up in the morning I found my host and hostess already in the dining room. It didn't take me long to join them for a delightful breakfast of fresh country eggs, bacon, and biscuits with real butter and homemade preserves. Mr. Gregory was enjoying retired life as a gentleman farmer. The Gregorys grew fresh vegetables, fruit trees, chickens, and cows that produced rich, creamy milk. Their pastures were beautiful, with many large trees and shrubs. Occasionally wild deer roamed through them. After breakfast Mr. Gregory took me for a tour around the farm and I fell in love with it. Before I left the peaches became ripe. They were so sweet and full of flavor that I have never since found a peach to equal them. My favorite peach specialty was the homemade peach ice cream made with fresh cream, but sliced peaches on my morning cereal and peach shortcake were also unbeatable. By the time I boarded the train to return to New York I was in good health and ready to get back to studies and work. I had to have a checkup before the doctor would let me go back to ward duty, but she gave me full clearance and told me to report to the nurse once a month to be weighed and checked.

All was well for several months. I had completed several services and enjoyed them all, but I found pediatrics and operating room my favorites. I was somewhat dismayed by neurosurgery. The Institute of Neurology was well known all over the world for advances in brain surgery, but I was quite discouraged by much that I saw. Patients undergoing a craniotomy were usually found to have advanced malignancies, since early detection was not available. The operations were very traumatic, lasting twelve or more hours. It was days before all the swelling was reduced and the patients regained any kind of consciousness. They were almost always paralyzed to some degree and unable to communicate effectively. At the time, I had to wonder if it was worthwhile. In fact, on my exit interview with the director of nurses at the institute, I was asked what I had learned from my experience. I described the many nursing interventions I had learned in order to make these patients as comfortable as possible. They required a great deal of support and nursing care. When I got through, the director looked at me and said, "Miss Davis, I am surprised that you didn't learn that if you have a brain tumor—for God's sake, keep it."

The prevention of infection is important no matter what the surgical intervention is, but before the discovery of antibiotics it was a constant concern. Bone infections were and still are very difficult to treat. During my rotation in the orthopedic operating room various methods were being tried to reduce the incidence of infection in the operating room. Ultraviolet lights were installed in the operating room to rid the air of airborne bacteria. The table on which all the instruments were set up for use during the case was made ready with a sterile canopy to keep dust from settling on the sterile field. The "scrub" nurse used sterile forceps to pick up all instruments before handing them to the surgeon. This could be quite difficult, because many of the orthopedic instruments were large and heavy. These instruments struck me as being very much like carpenters' tools. Since the ultraviolet lamps could cause severe sunburn, the circulating staff wore pith sun helmets and sunglasses as well as long sleeves.

During our training days we scrubbed for ten minutes with a brush of stiff bristles, using tincture of green soap, then took a handful of a chlorinated lime and rubbed it all over our hands and arms, which were already red and sore from scrubbing. After doing this we rinsed our arms in 70 percent alcohol. By this time, we were usually dancing a jig. Our arms felt as though they were on fire. I can remember shedding many a tear behind my mask. After going through this procedure several times a day there was no way that you could mask the smell of chlorine and alcohol. No one would ride on the elevator with us as we went off duty, nor would they sit with us at the dining room table. We wore our badge with a certain amount of pride, and I was sorry when my rotation through the operating room was over.

I didn't enjoy my rotation in obstetrics as much as some of the other services. As student nurses, we were permitted to do very little. "Twilight sleep" was being used and heralded as the "latest thing" in obstetrical anesthesia. The patients were first given a large dose of a barbiturate followed by morphine and scopolamine. The patients responded to pain, but afterward memory of pain was greatly reduced. The patients were totally irresponsible and climbed the wall, so a student was assigned to each patient to keep her from falling out of bed and being injured. We were not permitted to do rectal or vaginal exams, so we really didn't know how well a patient was progressing in labor and were just told to call the R.N. if we saw any blood or a presenting part. The babies were so blue and lethargic when born that I was frightened. The patients were so "out of it" that we did not experience any of the joy of a mother interacting with a newborn. Husbands were barely allowed to see their wives during the two-week hospital stay, and postpartum care was so routine that I was really bored by it.

We did no postpartum teaching, and the mothers were not permitted to do anything for themselves. Every four hours we pulled all the curtains around each bed and then started the bedpan routine. The sterilized bedpans were placed in paper bedpan covers and loaded onto a cart along with sterile pitchers containing a sterile antiseptic solution. We placed a paper bag containing five large cotton balls and a clean sterile perineal pad as well as a pair of sterile latex gloves on each over-the-bed table. After we had placed the patient on the bedpan and removed the soiled peripad, which was placed in another paper bag and disposed of in the large bag hanging on the cart, we then had to go to the sink at the end of the ward to scrub our hands for three minutes by the clock before returning to the patient to cleanse the perineum with the solution and cotton balls, apply the clean pad, then measure the contents of the bedpan and rinse the bedpan before placing it in the bedpan sterilizer.

The patients were bathed in bed each morning and their bed made up with clean linen. There were twelve patients on the ward, and usually one student had to service each one. I felt as though we no sooner got through with this routine before it was time to do it again. Every four hours we also had to go to the nursery for the cart of babies to be delivered to the mothers for nursing. Since the patients were not allowed to get out of bed for anything, all the food trays had to be passed and the patient cranked up in bed to eat (no electric beds in those days). There was no time to do anything but to hurry from one routine procedure to the next. I decided that I would never willingly take a job in an obstetrical unit. Little did I know that I would end up as a certified Maternal-gynecological-neonatal nurse and love it.

The early training I received did prepare me well for adjusting to changes in nursing and medical roles, and also for participating in the progress. In our senior year one of our rotations was in Harkness Pavilion, the private hospital frequented by many famous people. One afternoon

I looked out of the dormitory window to watch as President Franklin D. Roosevelt was wheeled into the hospital for a checkup. The hospital rooms were beautifully appointed and the meals very attractively served on huge trays with silver teapots and beautiful china. A fresh flower in a bud vase added to the appeal of the already attractive and appetizing food. As students, we could never serve one of these trays without dreaming of the day when we might be admitted to the floor reserved for nurses and physicians at the hospital. I had been having frequent attacks of severe abdominal pain and finally I did report to the infirmary. It was decided that I had appendicitis since my white count was elevated, with all the clinical indications. I was admitted to Harkness but given no food, since they were anticipating an appendectomy. After I had been under observation for about twelve hours another white count was taken, and since it had started to go down I was dismissed to return to the dormitory. I never did get to enjoy any of the wonderful food.

When I continued to have the abdominal pain from time to time, I timidly suggested that I might still be infected by the ameba I had acquired in China. I had been treated many times with Emetine while in China but apparently had become reinfected. The doctor reluctantly agreed to have a culture done. She really did not agree with my self-diagnosis, but a few days later I found a note in my mailbox saying, "You may go to the head of the class. You are infected with ameba. Report to the infirmary at once." I was confined to my room and given a can of disinfecting toilet cleaner to put in the toilet each time I went to the bathroom. I don't remember what drug I was put on, but after consulting with the Tropical Disease Committee I was given the prescribed number of pills and excused from duty until I had completed the course of medication.

Graduation took place in June of 1940, but since I missed time during my illness, I had to make that time up before I was eligible for state board exams. I was disappointed that I could not pack up my things, book passage to Manila, and be on my way to join my mother and dad. Actually, the experience of working on the wards as a graduate was good for me. I worked as a night float from 7 PM until 7 AM. Every night I worked on a different unit to relieve a nurse who had called in sick or where the work load had increased due to an emergency situation. I learned to adjust

Dorothy Davis, second from right, in June 1940, at graduation from Presbyterian Hospital School of Nursing, Columbia University. White stockings and cuffs (not visible in this photo) distinguished the nurses as new graduates. Davis was allowed to graduate with her class, but had to make up rotations she missed during illness before she could take state board exams.

rapidly and to know the routines of many services: orthopedics, general medicine, general or special surgery, genitourinary (GU), gastrointestinal (GI), and even the special research units. If all the wards were quiet, I was permitted to go to the "on call room" and sleep for a couple of hours. One night, just as I fell into a deep sleep, the nursing supervisor awakened me and told me that the nurse on the GU ward had become ill. The nurse was unable to stay to give me a report before she left, so when I took over it was up to me to find out something about each patient, as well as figure out what had been done and what still needed to be done. I decided that I needed to check each patient first, then worry about the paper work.

I found my first patient in a pool of blood and in shock. By the time I got the intern and he called the resident and we got the patient stabilized, it was after four in the morning. I still had several hours of work to do. Apparently the assigned nurse had been ill for her whole shift and had not started any of the routine charting or duties expected of the night nurse. Each chart had a front sheet that summarized total intake, output, all procedures, transfusions, temperature, pulse, respiration, blood pressure, and so on. Each medication given during the twenty-four-hour period had to be totaled and every lab report noted. Just getting the front sheets completed and ready for morning rounds took a lot of time. The night nurse was also expected to pass out wash water to each patient and help those who could not help themselves to at least wash hands and face and brush their teeth before breakfast trays arrived.

I was ready to give "report" by the time the day nurses arrived, and I left the unit feeling that I had done a pretty good job. I was tired and ready to go to bed and put the hectic night behind me, but no sooner had I reached my room when the buzzer rang to notify me that I had a call. I was told to report to the chief surgeon of the GU unit. The chief wanted to know why I had waited until the patient was in shock before calling the intern. I had charted the time of my arrival on the ward to take over and the time that I had found the patient and the action I had taken. I explained that I did not get a report from the off-going nurse, since she had left the unit before my arrival, so I could not ask any questions. If I didn't learn anything else by this experience, I did learn the importance of timely and accurate charting.

I learned a great deal during the six months that I had to make up. I probably learned more than I would have it I had spent the time during the regular training period. I was given more responsibility and more varied experiences than we had as students. By working so many different services throughout the hospital and being in a position where I had to rely on my own judgment, I soon lost my fear of something new.

The six months were finally up, and it was time to take state boards. This did frighten me. All questions were essay, and I found that I was writing pages and pages. I was glad it wasn't I who had to read and correct the handwritten papers. It would be several weeks before the results would be published, and I didn't want to wait for them before sailing to the Philippines to join my family.

I had expected to go back to China to work as a nurse, but the attack on Shanghai by the Japanese in 1937 shortly after my arrival in New York

City and changes imposed on trade in Shanghai made it impossible for my father to conduct business there. He and Mother had sold what they could and moved to Manila, Philippine Islands, where they started all over again. By the time I graduated from Presbyterian Hospital School of Nursing, Father's business was reestablished, and I booked passage on one of the Maersk freighters for Manila.

It was November 1940, and once again I packed my things in anticipation of a long voyage home. But this time home would be in Manila; I had no idea just what I would find when I arrived there. My parents had rented an apartment in Ermita, a suburb of Manila, and I could not remember much about the area from my earlier visits. They had left much of their furniture and the accumulation of treasures collected over the past thirty years in Shanghai, and I knew things would be different. I was saddened by the realization that I might never again see Shanghai, the city I had called home for nineteen years. However, there was no time to worry about the past; there was too much to look forward to.

I left Maxwell Hall, my home for almost four years, in a taxi on a cold, rainy November afternoon. When I arrived at the dock in lower Manhattan, the freighter looked dwarfed amid the larger passenger ships and the busy port activities. I was the only passenger to board the ship, and not long after I was settled in my comfortable cabin, the ship's whistles sounded and I could feel the ship roll and pitch. I looked out of the porthole and could see that the water had become very rough. We were passing Cape Hatteras, and I remembered being told that the sea is often rough at that point. Although I had been through some rough seas, I had never experienced such motion before. Each time the stern of the ship came up, the propellers came out of the water, causing the ship to vibrate and shimmy. Then it would roll over to the side, and the sea would appear to rush towards the porthole. Just as I was sure we would capsize, the ship would lurch and start moving in another direction. I was unable to do anything but head for my bunk and pray that we would stay afloat and that we would survive. I had never experienced severe seasickness before. I now knew what it was like, and I have never since lacked sympathy with anyone experiencing the malady.

As long as I remained prone, with my eyes closed, I was fairly comfortable, but soon there was a knock on my cabin door. It was the steward saying that dinner was being served and the captain would like me to join him and the other officers at their table. I told him that I was not hungry and declined. He left but was soon back, urging me once again to come to the dining room. I was too proud to admit that I was seasick and just couldn't make it, so I got up and staggered to the dining room. I was feeling so badly that I had made no effort to clean up or to change my clothes. I did manage to get to the table, but the minute I looked at and smelled the rich Danish meal spread on the table, I got up and bolted to my cabin, where I flopped on the bunk and did not move until the next morning. When I awakened, the ship was moving normally and the sun was shining through the porthole. I wasn't sure that I hadn't died and gone to heaven.

I was starved, so I got up, bathed and dressed, then headed for the deck to test my stomach and convince myself that all was well. I felt great. Breakfast was being served, so I made my way to the dining room and ate an enormous breakfast, never admitting that I had been seasick the night before. I am sure that I didn't fool anyone, but the crew was most gracious and didn't tease me about it. I found that the only other passenger at that time had boarded the night before and was still indisposed and had not left his cabin. He did not leave his cabin until we reached Panama, where he disembarked. Fortunately, I did not become seasick again and was able to enjoy the next six weeks at sea.

I didn't have a roommate until we arrived in San Diego. At first I thought that the young lady I was to share the cabin with would be a pleasant companion, but it turned out that she was planning to marry a man who said he was going to divorce his wife and marry her. She told me every detail of her clandestine affair. It was more than I wanted to know, but I couldn't turn her off. She told me he had paid for her ticket to Manila and she was looking forward to a happy life with him. A few days after arrival in Manila she called me and hysterically told me that he was not going to marry her, that he had beat her up and now she was going to commit suicide. My sister, who had returned to Manila with my mother soon after my father had reestablished business and found a place to live, went with me to her hotel room. We managed to calm her down enough to get her to a doctor, where she was sedated and admitted to the hospital for psychiatric evaluation.

Another passenger who tested my newly acquired nursing skills was a young woman who spent quite a bit of time with the captain. She suffered from migraine headaches, and one evening she was in so much pain that she was banging her head against the wall and screaming. Aspirin did nothing to ease the pain. I consulted the captain, who was responsible for medical care when there was no doctor on the ship. He agreed that the woman should be sedated. He unlocked the medication cabinet. I found that the only medication strong enough to relieve the pain was morphine. At that time morphine was the drug of choice since none of the synthetic drugs had yet been discovered.

I prepared a suitable dose for a woman of her weight and gave her a shot. Since I had medicated her with a narcotic, I felt I should spend the night with her. I left her with the captain long enough to go back to my cabin to get the things I would need for the night. When I returned, her respirations had dropped to less than ten per minute. I was very concerned—morphine was a respiratory depressant—and told the captain that this was a symptom of overdose, but I couldn't believe that the dose I had given her could have caused the problem. I spent the entire night stimulating her and telling her to take deep breaths.

By morning she was responsive and asking for breakfast. Two weeks after arriving in Manila the lady called me to tell me that after I had left her cabin to get my things, the captain had given her another dose of morphine. Although I had told him that I was worried because I felt she had received an overdose of morphine, he never told me that he had given her more medication.

This trip certainly had been different from the carefree trip I had taken to New York four years earlier. I began to realize that I would be taking on more and more responsibilities as time went on.

As the ship made its way slowly past Corregidor Island and into beautiful Manila Bay, the heat and humidity were oppressive, but the tropical flora and scenery were beautiful. As the harbor tugs took their places against the hull of the ship to nudge it up against the dock, I could see my mother and dad waiting. I was relieved to see them looking well and happy. Weekly letters from my mother had reassured me that all was well with them and that they were recovering from the financial losses and other stresses of being relocated. I was glad that I would not have to go through customs. (Manila was under the jurisdiction of the United States as a commonwealth nation). As soon as the gangway was in place I left the ship to join my family. After a joyful and tearful reunion, my father made arrangements for my baggage and we were on our way.

I was anxious to get a job and immediately set out to see what I would have to do in order to be registered in the Philippines. I was registered in New York, which was recognized in every other state in the United States, but my license was not recognized in the Philippines even though it was a commonwealth of the United States. It seemed that the New York Board of Nurse Examiners would not give the Philippines reciprocity, so the Philippines would not accept New York's registration. I would have to take the exams again. Fortunately I did not have to wait six months as I had in New York, since the biannual exam was to be given in Manila in less than two weeks. I registered for the exam and, while I waited for the appointed time, I became acquainted with the social life of Manila. The army and navy dependents had been sent back to the States because of the rumblings of impending war with the Japanese, but the remaining population of Americans did not act as though there were any truth to the rumors. It was business as usual.

I don't remember all my dates, but I do remember my first date. I met the young man at the Polo Club just a few days after my arrival. He had grown up in Manila and was the oldest son of a prominent Manila family. We had dinner at the Manila Hotel,where he had ordered flowers for the table and a special dinner with baked Alaska for dessert. He was obviously well known at the hotel, and the waiter was very attentive. I was really impressed and enjoyed the attention. We danced under the stars until the curfew at 11 PM closed the nightclub.

While I was waiting to take the nursing board exams, I learned that Sternberg General Hospital, the army hospital in Manila, was hiring Civil Service nurses. All that was required was a valid passport and a nursing license from any state in the United States. I applied for a Civil Service

Dorothy Davis, third from right, at her first dance at the Polo Club in Manila, December 1940.

commission in the U.S. Army and was hired, pending the usual reference checks and a physical. U.S. Army installations were, and still are, considered federal property and are not subject to local jurisdiction.

Since I had already paid the registration fee for the Philippine board exams, and I had not yet started my job at Sternberg General Hospital, I decided to go ahead and take the exams. It wouldn't hurt to be registered in the Philippines if I later decided to work in a local civilian hospital. The format for the exams seemed to be similar to those in New York. Each exam would take two hours, followed by a practical exam. I was surprised when I found all the exams were true/false or multiple-choice questions. It took me fifteen minutes to complete each exam, even though I checked my answers twice. I had over an hour and a half between each exam to kill. I spent my time knitting. On the third day I was approached by one of the teachers, who asked me if I was having trouble with the exams. He thought I had been unable to answer the questions and was skipping most of them. He wondered why I was not studying as the other nurses were doing if they finished early. I was having a hard time understanding why it took most of them two hours to complete such easy exams. Each of the New York essay exams had taken me every bit of two hours. I began to doubt myself. Was I missing something on the Philippine exam? I was greatly relieved when the results were published and I had passed, although by that time I had already started to work at Sternberg General Hospital.

My first assignment at Sternberg was on the obstetrical ward, where my orientation lasted one morning. No babies were born that day, so I never did observe the routines used. The next day I was to work the 1 PM to 7 PM shift by myself. All the American dependents had been sent back to the United States as a precaution, but the Philippine Scout wives stationed at Fort McKinley were still receiving care at Sternberg. I was told that if a patient was admitted in labor, I should call the officer-of-the-day (OD) for the delivery. I was not told that the OD might be a dentist or a psychiatrist who had not attended a delivery since medical school, or that the doctor had no intention of arriving in time for the delivery. He would eventually arrive to sign the birth certificate.

My first patient arrived at 4 PM and delivered at 4:10 PM I had time to put on one glove and to put a sterile sheet under the patient's buttocks. The baby emerged screaming his little head off and mama seemed very pleased, although I didn't understand a word of the Tagalog she was speaking. Since I was the only employee on duty, I had to take care of the baby, settle the mother in her room, and also clean the delivery room and prepare it for the next delivery. By the time I had taken care of the baby and returned to check on my patient I found that she had already gotten out of bed and emptied her bladder. And she had not used any cleansing solution! I had been taught to keep obstetrical patients in bed for ten days, and our patients in New York had not been permitted to take care of their own hygienic needs. The nurse provided all care, using sterile techniques to avoid infection.

I felt that I had failed my patient and worried about her until I came back on duty the next afternoon and found her happily nursing her baby and planning to take him home the next day. In the States, obstetrical patients were pampered even after they returned home, so I was surprised to find the Filipino women doing so well with early ambulating.

One day I was transferred to the officers' medical ward. That day, a young officer named Don Childers was being discharged to quarters following a bout with pneumonia. He was tall, dark, and handsome with a winning personality, and I immediately "fell" for him. When he asked if he could call me at home, I saw no reason to say no. I certainly did not know that in a few months we would become engaged to be married.

We had a date every evening unless one or both of us were on duty. Sometimes we had dinner with my parents, then went out dancing, usually at the Army Navy Club, but occasionally we would go to the Club Jai-lai, where we could have dinner and dance or watch jai-lai, the fast Spanish court game. We could sit in the viewing area in comfortable chairs or at the dinner table to watch the game from the glassed-in viewing area, or we could dance the night away.

Regardless of the shift I was assigned to—7 AM to 1 PM, 1 PM to 7 PM, or 7 PM to 7 AM—I would find time to ride, play badminton or tennis, or swim. However, I didn't care for the night shift because it interfered with my night life. This pleasant life continued and we tended to ignore the modest but observable increase in military presence in Manila. Don and I set a target date for our wedding as the spring of 1942.

By September 1941, the army dependents had been gone for almost a year and the expected hostilities had not materialized, so reduction of nursing staff at Sternberg General Hospital was ordered. This meant that the most recently hired Civil Service nurses would be the first to go. After working for only eight months, I suddenly found myself unemployed. I had already taken my physical exam and completed my application to join the Army Nurse Corps, but all the paper work had to go to Washington, D.C., for processing and approval. Mail was sent by ship and nothing happened quickly. There was nothing to do but wait.

Just before losing my job, I had purchased a horse for one hundred dollars, a very low price for a good horse. He had been one of the cavalry horses but had earned a very poor reputation, since none of the men could control him. I heard that he was to be destroyed as unsafe and unfit. I asked how much they would get for his carcass and when they told me fifty dollars, I offered one hundred. I had a hard time convincing the commanding officer that I could manage the horse called Napo, but they decided to let me try.

I missed my work at the hospital, but now I had more time to work with Napo. I discovered that most of his rebelliousness was caused by friction on his back and withers from the saddle. I found a saddle that would not rub, and since I weighed about half as much as the soldiers I was able to make him much more comfortable. The soldiers had been trying to control him by brute force, and I knew that this would not work for me, so we started out very slowly taking leisurely walks. I used a very light rein that didn't irritate him. The pain caused by the rider pulling and sawing the reins had infuriated him. A horse is always stronger than the strongest man, and if the horse becomes sufficiently agitated, the rider will be on the losing side. I was careful not to excite him until he gained confidence in me and knew he would not be hurt. By the end of the first week I could let him extend to a full gallop and stop him on command. I could ride him right by the very noisy airplane engines that were being tested. He would not shy away or start to dance and prance. Most of the horses would become very agitated and sometimes the rider would lose control. The noise was deafening and could easily upset any animal.

I felt Napo was ready to join a group of officers who had organized a Sunday morning cross-country recreational ride. I asked permission for us to do so. I had been told that Napo was not welcome on these rides since he had always disturbed the other horses and had caused many a "run away." I was finally given permission to join but was told to stay well away from the other riders. The first ride went without incident until we came to a deep and wide ditch where the horses had to slide down one side then climb up the other side. The leading horse refused to go, and one by one the other horses followed the example of the first horse. I finally came forward and asked permission to lead the group across. The captain couldn't believe that I would even consider trying, since Napo was usually the one to create this kind of problem. The captain laughingly and rather sarcastically said to go ahead. Napo calmly slid down the embankment and up the other side without a trace of reluctance, and all the other horses followed along. After that, Napo and I were both allowed to join any group that rode the range.

Career in the Making

4 | World War II in the Philippines

I was having a wonderful time and ignored any talk of building tensions. Convoys and trucks were moving in and out of the city, loaded with airplane parts and weapons of all kinds, and rumors were rampant. Even though Don was spending more time in the field, we continued to see each other almost every night. Manila had been under an 11 PM curfew for months, so we just took it for granted that Don would escort me home in time for him to make it back to Fort McKinley by 11 PM.

Sunday morning Don called to tell me that he would pick me up for our planned picnic at Lake Taal. Joe Iacalucci, another officer assigned to the 57th Infantry, and Phyllis Arnold, one of the army nurses, would join us. Don said that we would have to return early since he and Joe had to be back at Fort McKinley by 5 PM. It was a beautiful day and we enjoyed every minute of it. We sang all the old favorites we could remember as we drove home. I was still glowing with happiness when Don brought me home. I am sure now that he knew more about what was going on than Phyllis or I did, but both Joe and he were determined not to spoil the afternoon. We had been complacent about the possibility of hostilities for

First Lieutenant Donald Childers, the author's fiancé (second from left), and his housemates in bivouac, shortly before they departed for Bataan, December 1941.

months; however, I believe most of us knew that the situation was becoming tense. Monday morning I awakened still thinking of the great time we had enjoyed and looking forward to seeing Don again that evening.

At that very hour, however, Don's unit was preparing to leave Manila for Bataan. I would never see him again.

Manila Harbor was one of the finest natural harbors in the world. The entrance to the bay, thirty miles west of Manila, was twelve miles wide and bounded on the north by the large, mountainous Bataan Peninsula. Fortress Corregidor, two miles from Bataan, along with two small fortified islands farther to the south, controlled access to its entrance channels. Sangley Point, with its Cavite Naval Yard, home of our Far East fleet, jutted out from the southern shore only five miles from Manila.

I prefer to remember Bataan as I saw it so long ago, as Don and I walked along the beach or enjoyed a cool tall drink and watched the gorgeous tropical sunset from the beach next to the Army Navy Club. I loved to see the sun sink behind Mount Mariveles, Bataan's principal mountain, and watch the colors change from brilliant reds, oranges, and yellows to

The Philippines, 1942–45

PHILIPPINE SEA

Cape Engano

Aparri
Vigan
Tuguegarao
Santo Tomas
Kiangan
Baguio
Lingayen

LUZON

Iba
Capas
San Fernando

Subic Bay
Bataan
Manila
Mariveles
Mauban
Atimonan

SOUTH CHINA SEA

MINDORO

Legaspi

San Bernardino Strait

SamJose

Masbate

SAMAR

PANAY

Tacloban
Palo
Ormoc
Dulag
Leyte Gulf

LEYTE

Iloilo

Cebu

PALAWAN

Puerto Princesa

Negros

SULU SEA

Cagayan

MINDANAO

Cotabato
Davao

Zamboanga

somber purples, and gradually fade into darkness. Sometimes the colors would extend to overhead and beyond, so one felt actually in the midst of the sunset, surrounded by all the changing colors. Sometimes the sky would be serene and peaceful, and then again it might turn angry and wild as a tropical storm suddenly appeared. One of the first folklore tales told to new arrivals in the Philippines is the story about the formation of Mount Mariveles: As the sun sets behind the mountain, the silhouette of a beautiful lady can be imagined lying on her back, her breasts jutting skyward and her long hair flowing into the sea.

It was still Sunday, 7 December in Hawaii, although it was Monday, 8 December in Manila. We were shocked to learn that Pearl Harbor had been bombed by the Japanese around 7 AM Hawaii time, 2 AM Monday morning in Manila. Rumors were that we would be next!

By the time I knew what had happened to Don's unit, the 57th Infantry Philippine Scouts, he was already on the way to Bataan. I knew that Corregidor's huge coast artillery batteries controlled the bay, but I didn't know the importance of Bataan in making Corregidor almost impregnable. The Japanese couldn't begin to attack Corregidor without first occupying Bataan so they could line up their vast quantity of field artillery, blast Corregidor to pieces, and prepare to launch their amphibious attack. This is why the Philippine Scouts, our very best troops, were immediately rushed to secure Bataan. The only bright spot in my day was a note from Don written on a scrap of paper and delivered by a man who could not tell me where it had come from. It was written in the field, and Don said that he already missed me and hoped to return to Manila for a day or so soon.

Before daylight on Tuesday, 9 December, we were awakened by the sounds of many bombers flying over the city followed by the wailing air raid sirens and the sound of bombs exploding. This attack resulted in the loss of most of the airplanes at Nichols Field, which was just a short distance from my parent's apartment. My family and I, along with all the others living in the Ermita apartment building, made our way down to the basement, where we huddled until daybreak. The bombing soon stopped, but I knew there must have been casualties and Sternberg Hospital would need every available nurse. I put my uniform on and made my way to the hospital; I was quickly reinstated as a Civil Service nurse, assigned to Sternberg Hospital, and put to work.

I didn't know that Clark Field was also bombed at high noon the day before, with many casualties and virtually all planes destroyed. Fortunately, half of our own recently arrived Flying Fortresses (B-17s) had been sent to Del Monte on Mindanao Island and would be safe for the moment. They later operated from Australia. The many soldiers wounded at Clark Field received only first aid before being sent by train to Sternberg.

My first assignment was to set up a fifty-bed unit and to be ready to admit more wounded from Clark Field. The first trainload of patients from Clark arrived at 2 AM, filling most of the available beds at Sternberg (Santo Scolastica, an annex to Sternberg, was also receiving patients). However, more beds were needed at Sternberg to receive the second trainload of patients, which would arrive at 4 PM and were to be admitted to an unused enlisted personnel housing area on the second floor. I found a vacated area in one wing of the hospital and realized that I had a lot of work to do if we expected to be ready on time. Cots had been moved in, but nothing else. No one told me how to go about getting the things I would need to transform this dormitory arrangement into a nursing unit with all the supplies and medications that would be needed to care for wounded. I started by trying to think of all the things I would expect to find if I were assigned to care for patients already in the unit.

To begin with, there was no phone or any other means of communication. I found a sergeant who looked friendly and asked him where to start. He said he could make the necessary arrangements to have a phone installed, but he had no idea what a nurse would need in order to care for the expected wounded soldiers. He said he could find some bed linen and a few enlisted men to make up the beds. This was a start, and we would at least get a patient in a bed. The patients would also need medications, dressings, treatment equipment, hygiene supplies, vital sign monitoring equipment, forms, and so on.

I found a cart and headed for the quartermaster supply building. Everyone was busy, so I decided I would help myself to what I needed. When I was ready to leave, with my cart piled high, I was asked for six copies of the requisition listing everything I had picked up. I didn't even have a scrap of paper to give him, and furthermore, I had no intention of filling out any forms. My patients would be arriving any minute, and I was sure they would need care more than the supply lieutenant needed requisitions. I left the second lieutenant in a state of total frustration, but I had the unit ready in time. My conscience really didn't bother me too much and would have bothered me even less had I known then that the entire hospital would disappear in a heap of rubble when Manila was freed from Japanese occupation three and a half years later.

The following day, Wednesday, 11 December, four or five formations of two-engine Japanese bombers circled Manila, flying above twenty thousand feet. American antiaircraft shells could not reach above ten thousand feet, so the shells exploded harmlessly in the air. After a half hour of circling around Manila, they concentrated their bombing on Nichols Field and Cavite Naval Yard, virtually destroying everything. After this, things became relatively quiet, with only sporadic dive bombing by small groups of a few planes. They seemed to be concentrating on military targets largely outside of Manila proper. Most of us, not knowing what to expect, took cover every time we heard a plane overhead. One day, as I squatted under a building during a raid, almost paralyzed with anxiety, a feeling of calm took over and I felt that there was no need to worry. Our lives were in the Lord's hands, and "what would be would be." For the first time since the attack on Manila had started, I was able to go calmly about my work.

Things were not going well. Japanese planes were overhead daily. At first when we heard the sound of planes we thought they might be ours, but we soon learned from the patients streaming into the hospital that we had virtually no planes left to defend us. Nichols Field was destroyed. The cavalry had left, taking the horses with them. I found out later that Napo had been left behind, tied to a fence. By the time the U.S. forces surrendered in Bataan, all of the cavalry horses had been eaten by our starving troops. I don't know what happened to Napo. Perhaps he became the mount for some high-ranking Japanese officer.

Extra cots were set up in the nurse's quarters for the civilian nurses who lived in the city. We slept when we could, which wasn't often. I was assigned to night duty, which technically ran from 7 PM to 7 AM. At night we had to work under blackout conditions. Since there was no air conditioning, hanging heavy drapes over the windows would have made the already hot air unbearable. So we were permitted to use a flashlight covered by a piece of red paper. This helped us move about without running into things but did not provide enough light to read, mix, and calculate medication doses. Morphine tablets came as ½ g or 1 g tablets and had to be mixed in 1 cc of distilled water, brought to a boil in a spoon held over a flame before being drawn into a syringe, and administered to the patient. Flames were forbidden after dark, so even if we could have seen well enough to prepare the narcotic, we would not have been able to sterilize the medication for hypodermic administration. My solution for this problem was to report to work at 4:30 PM. I would eat supper before reporting to my assigned area, prepare the medications, and place the syringes on a tray covered by a sterile towel. Then I made rounds to check each patient so that I could develop some kind of a nursing care plan before darkness fell.

I never felt that I was giving my patients as much care as they deserved. Some nights I was responsible for over a hundred patients. I never would have made it without the help of the ambulatory patients. The patients who could move about at all would help less fortunate patients by getting them water, helping them move into a more comfortable position, or sometimes just sitting by a cot and holding a hand. I could always depend on one of the volunteers to let me know when a patient needed more than he could handle. I remember one young man in particular who was a patient in the hospital when the war started. He was a "goldbrick," feigning injury or illness in order to escape work. He wanted to be sent back to the States and insisted that his knee hurt too much for him to work. The day the Japanese bombed Manila he threw away his cane, stopped limping, and was one of my most dedicated helpers. When needed, he stayed up all night. I often wondered if he ever got home. So few of my friends did!

We were always listening for the sound of planes overhead and the now-familiar sound of sirens. As the Japanese had complete control of the air, they limited their air activity to daylight hours. When I was relieved in the morning, I would go to the nurses' quarters for breakfast and then try to get some sleep. If lucky, I could sleep for an hour or two before the Japanese would start their intermittent bombing. There were no bomb shelters. The hospital consisted of two-story wood buildings arranged in a quadrangle, with the operating rooms in the center. Many of the buildings were old Spanish barracks with a second story added by the Americans. Zig zag trenches were dug in the grassy areas, and we were instructed to get all the ambulatory patients into the trenches each time the air raid sirens sounded. The ambulatory patients were housed on the second floor. There were no elevators, and it was not easy for patients in casts to get down the stairs. Patients helped each other, and, with the adrenaline flowing, most of them made it to the trenches, but when the all-clear sounded we often had difficulty getting everyone back to bed. On 23 December Manila was declared an open city. General MacArthur had decided to pull the military out of Manila so that the Japanese would refrain from bombing the city and killing innocent men, women, and children. The Japanese wanted the city for their own, and they also wanted the Filipinos to believe that Japan had attacked the Philippine Islands to free the Filipinos from United States domination. Our plan was to defend the Philippines from Corregidor and Bataan after a delaying action of Japanese landings well north and south of Manila. Therefore, the 31st Infantry of the Philippine Scouts had left the city soon after the first Japanese attack on 8 December. Only the hospital and noncombat troops remained in Manila. Any U.S. military combat soldiers found in Manila once the Japanese entered the city more than likely would be shot.

Most of us did not know anything about plans for defending the city, and we had no business knowing; however, we were all becoming anxious. We heard many rumors about the approaching Japanese troops. Lack of sleep and no time away from work began to take its toll. Conversations and questions about what would happen if reinforcements didn't arrive were frequent as we sat at the dinner table. One of the civilian nurses made the comment that she didn't have to worry about being impregnated by a Japanese soldier if she were raped, since she was already pregnant. Her husband had left the city with the troops to defend the

Philippines. He never saw his baby son, who was born while his mother was an internee.

I continued to ask our commanding officer if he had received any information regarding my application for the Army Nurse Corps. His answer was always negative. I had hoped to hear from the surgeon general before the army moved out of Manila; however, my commanding officer told me that I would not be permitted to leave Manila with the army nurses unless my commission came through and I could be sworn into the army before the last group left.

At dusk on 24 December, Christmas Eve, all American medical personnel, physicians, dentists, nurses, and enlisted corps men were moved to the jungles of Bataan, where Hospital Number 2, a huge field hospital, was being set up to care for sick and wounded soldiers. A skeleton American staff consisting of four physicians, one dentist, one surgical nurse, one medical service officer, and two American civilian nurses remained at Sternberg: one nurse for 7 AM to 7 PM, and one nurse for the night shift, 7 PM to 7 AM. A few Filipino nurses and enlisted men were added to this count to care for the seven hundred patients still at Sternberg Hospital. I made rounds as often as I could to oversee the care given by the Filipino nurses, who had received no orientation and therefore did not know where to find anything; nor did they know how to follow the orders written by the doctors. One evening I arrived on a unit to find the newly admitted soldiers still in their battle uniforms dirty and bloody. When I asked the nurses why they had not cleaned up the men, their answer was, "But, Mum, there are no pajamas." I showed them where to find pajamas, which were in the linen closet, and tried to make them understand that they had to use a little initiative. Even if no pajamas had been available, they should have cleaned the men up and covered them with a sheet. I was more upset because I had found the nurses huddled in the nurses' station doing nothing. Each evening when I reported to work around 4:30 PM, I found that some of the less injured patients had been moved by motor convoy to the new field hospital in Bataan, but progress was slow, and by the end of December there were still some two hundred patients in Sternberg Hospital.

Christmas came and went. Now it was New Year's Eve and I hadn't been home to see my parents or sister but once since the war started. On the morning of 31 December, after I came off my night shift, I felt I must touch base with them to be sure they were all right.

Since all transportation had been commandeered by the army, to be used for evacuation of military personnel out of the city, I had to walk home. We lived about three miles away. I started home, and I was awed by the eerie appearance of the city. The last two days before the Japanese entered Manila, looting was allowed at the abandoned military sites. It was better for the Filipinos to get the supplies and equipment left behind than to allow the Japanese to get it. People came with trucks, pony cars, wagons, even wheelbarrows, and loaded up. I was so exhausted I felt I was floating along the deserted streets. I had to step over debris and occasionally detour around blocked areas, but I finally arrived at the apartment.

Mother welcomed me with open arms and, in spite of our need and desire to talk, she could see that I was too tired to make sense. She put me straight to bed. I fell asleep immediately, but that day the planes started bombing again, and they seemed to be getting much too close for comfort. With each explosion I would wake up, but my mother was always sitting by my bed, reassuring me that she would let me know if we should go to the basement, which was used as a shelter. I slept until about 1 PM and felt rested for the first time in three weeks. I took a wonderful hot shower, changed into fresh, clean clothes, ate a sandwich and bowl of soup, then headed back to the hospital.

When I got back to Sternberg, late in the afternoon, I found almost all of the patients gone, with only a few Filipino patients remaining. As darkness descended I felt deserted. I was alone with only the six officer medical personnel left in the hospital.

I didn't know that this group of officers had been appointed to supervise the evacuation of the patients, nor did I know where or how they were going to leave. All I knew was that I was being left alone to take care of the few remaining patients. I was angry when I realized that they were leaving. I had received no orders, and I didn't know what was expected of me. No one seemed to know, but Roy Bodine, a dental officer, did come back to my wards and try to cheer me up and offer some support. It was after midnight when their transportation arrived, and I waved goodbye to Roy and the other five officers.

I had not been relieved of duty, and the Filipina nurses assigned to take care of the remaining Filipino patients asked me to stay. I spent the rest of the night wandering through the now almost deserted hospital. During the last three and a half weeks of working nights I had looked forward to daylight. Whenever possible, I would go out on the balcony to watch the sun come up and see the American flag being raised while a recording of the "Star Spangled Banner" broke the morning silence. When the sun came up that last morning, the flag did not go up, and there was no one there to play the recording. It was New Years Day, 1942! I quietly left and walked home to the sound of approaching Japanese troops.

5 | Freedom Lost

As I slowly walked home, I wondered what would happen next. I had the feeling that I was in another world. Nothing looked familiar. The streets were deserted. In the distance occasional gunfire and the rumbling of heavy equipment could be heard. I was afraid I would find no one at my parents' apartment. To my relief I found everyone safe and sound. I would not be alone. We all started to talk, but no one had any answers to the one question that haunted each of us: "Would we be taken prisoners?" If so, when, and where would we be taken? Perhaps we would be allowed to stay in our homes. The family agreed that we should stock up on as much nonperishable food as possible. Mother had been keeping a reasonably good supply of canned food in the house since the hostilities had started, but she sent Hilario, our houseboy, to the market to purchase what he could. When he returned he reported all the rumors rampant on the street. Some were saying that everybody would be killed, while others said that civilians would be allowed to stay in their homes.

There was nothing to do but wait. Mother packed all the silver and valuables in trunks. We tried to keep occupied with busy work, but it was hard to get very enthusiastic about anything, wondering about our fate. At least the guns had been silenced. Finally, on the fourth day, Japanese trucks started to rumble through the streets giving instructions through loudspeakers to all United States citizens and allies. We were to pack three days' supply of food and clothes and be ready to be picked up in thirty minutes. We were to be taken to a place where we would be registered. I don't remember the term "internee" (nonmilitary persons captured by an invading country) being used at the time, but regardless of the terminology, it was clear that we were not free to do as we pleased. We were herded like animals by the Japanese military, who seemed determined to show us "who was boss."

Since we would have to carry our own suitcases, we decided to limit the personal effects and clothes to the barest minimum, so we could take more heavy cans of food. Fortunately, the weather in the Philippines is always warm, so we didn't have to burden ourselves with heavy clothing.

The registration point turned out to be Rizal Stadium, where we found most of our friends along with other Allied civilians. There appeared to be no organization, and everyone was milling about exchanging rumors. Most people thought that, since we had been told we would only need a three-day supply of food and clothes, we would be released to go home as soon as everyone was registered. If we had known that we would never again see our homes or most of the things we had left behind, we would have been much more upset than we were. Just as it began to get dark we were herded into buses and taken to Santo Tomas University.

Shortly after Japanese troops had invaded the Philippines, the Philippine army had commandeered the university buildings to house Filipino troops. Most of the furniture had been removed, and no effort had been made to clean up the mess that the troops had left. Most of the classrooms were empty and dirty. A few of the rooms did have double-deck army cots with dirty mattresses left by the Philippine troops, but no bedding.

Women and children were sent to one area and the men to another; no families were permitted to stay together. Depending on the size of the room, twenty-five to forty-five persons were assigned to each room. Since there were so few beds, and most of us had not brought any bedding into the camp, many slept on the bare concrete floor that night. There were no showers and very few wash sinks in the public toilets, and we were already feeling dirty, disheveled, and exhausted. We had been taken to Rizal Stadium at about 11:30 AM and it was now 7 or 8 PM.

No plans had been made to provide a place to eat for us or to prepare the food that we brought with us. I don't even remember if we tried to fix anything that first night. After we were assigned a room, we were told that at 9 PM we were to line up for roll call. We stood in line for some time while we waited our turn to be counted, with still no idea of what to expect. Finally, a soldier marched into the room with the ever-present sword clashing in its scabbard. We were ordered to bow; then roll call was taken. We were told that this routine would be carried out each evening at 9 PM.

The lights were turned off and there was nothing to do but try to get some sleep. I decided to make myself as comfortable as possible on the floor. I used some of my clothing for a pillow and did manage to get some sleep. The mosquitoes found me, and I was getting sore from lying on the hard concrete floor, so I was glad to see daylight. Very early I found quite a few people wandering around the halls. I searched the halls until I found my sister and mother, but we did not know which room my father had been assigned to. He eventually found us and together we tried to fix breakfast. There were no stoves to heat anything and no refrigerators to keep food from spoiling and being invaded by insects. Since there were four of us, we could open one can and finish it before it spoiled. Many however, tried to save food to eat later, so it was just a few hours before the bathrooms were filled with internees with diarrhea and vomiting.

I seemed to be the only nurse around. It was soon apparent that the Japanese would do nothing to organize the camp or create any order. Some of the civic leaders from Manila got together to form a committee and organize a plan that would keep everybody busy and out of trouble. We felt that, if we could control our own people, the Japanese would not be as likely to use their military tactics to keep us in line. I offered to do what I could to provide nursing care for the rapidly increasing number of sick people. Several doctors came forward and also offered their services. The doctors and I decided that we should try to find a room where we

IN REPLY REFER TO S. G. O. _____

WAR DEPARTMENT
OFFICE OF THE SURGEON GENERAL
WASHINGTON

March 18, 1942

Mrs. Carroll R. Hutchins
156 Amory Street
Brookline, Mass.

My dear Mrs. Hutchins:

Your letter of March 16, 1942, to Major Julia Stimson has
been received.

We are sorry that we can give you no definite information
about your niece Dorothy S. Davis. We know that she was on duty at
Sternberg Hospital and were about to appoint her to the Army Nurse
Corps when hostilities broke out. We were then unable to get orders
to her so we do not know what her status is at the present time.

I am sorry I am unable to give you a more definite reply.

Very truly yours,

Julia O. Flikke m
Colonel, A. U. S.
Superintendent, ANC

*The United States War Department's response to a letter of inquiry from the author's aunt, Dora
Hutchins, as to the author's whereabouts after hostilities broke out in Manila 8 December 1941.*

WAR DEPARTMENT
SERVICES OF SUPPLY
OFFICE OF THE PROVOST MARSHAL GENERAL
WASHINGTON

October 9, 1942

Mrs. W. J. Howes,

Liberty Corner, New Jersey.

Dear Mrs. Howes:

The Provost Marshal General has directed me to reply further to your inquiry of September 28, 1942, in regard to Mr. and Mrs. A. C. Davis, Miss Eva Grace Davis and Miss Dorothy Davis.

This office has received unofficial information that A. C. Davis, Mrs. A. C. Davis, Miss Dorothy Davis and Miss Eva Grace Davis have been interned by Japan at Santo Tomas, Manila. This office cannot be certain that these are the same persons about whom you inquired.

Communications may be addressed to A. C. Davis, Mrs. A. C. Davis, Miss Dorothy Davis, and Miss Eva Grace Davis by following the inclosed instructions. There is, however, no assurance that delivery can be effected in Japanese controlled areas at this time.

If the above-mentioned names appear on further information received by this office, you will be notified.

Sincerely yours,

Howard F. Bresee,
Lt. Col., C.M.P.,
Chief, Information Bureau.

1 Incl.
    Info. Cir.

FOR VICTORY
BUY
UNITED STATES
WAR
BONDS
AND
STAMPS

The United States War Department's response to a letter of inquiry from Mrs. W. J. Howe, the author's aunt (Grace Ellen Anderson Howe), as to the status of Dorothy Davis and her immediate family. One of a series of inquiries made by the author's aunts and uncles.

could set up a clinic, so I immediately set out to find one that was not occupied. We were given no guidance from the Japanese, so I just picked a vacant room.

No one could tell me whom I should ask for permission, so I gathered together as many volunteers as I could to help me clean a room and look for a few chairs and a table. We started without any supplies or medications. Later, I found out that the doctors did have a few medications, which they would provide as soon a we had a safe place to keep them. Every time we thought we were at the point where we could put a clinic sign on the door, the Japanese would arrive with a new group of internees and take our clean room away from us. We moved six times!

During this period, the camp committee decided that all alcoholic beverages should be confiscated. Each room was inspected, and all the "booze" was given to me for use in the clinic for medicinal purposes. Consensus of the medical staff was that most of it should be poured down the drain. We had no place to lock up anything, so it would be only too easy for the Japanese soldiers to find the medicinal alcohol and either drink it themselves or punish us for having it. We certainly did not want them to be under the influence any more than we wanted the internees to get out of control.

Until we had a place where people could go when they needed medical attention, I made rounds looking for those who needed help. My first patient turned out to be the wife of a man who had confided in me during our trip from New York to the Philippines more than a year earlier. He had told me then that his wife was suffering from schizophrenia and was hospitalized. He had hoped that she would recover enough to join him, but he was concerned that if trouble started she might not be able to handle it. I didn't know that she had come to Manila to join her husband. Once I met her it was obvious to me that she should not have come. She was in an extremely agitated condition, and her roommates were alarmed. Apparently her condition had improved while at the hospital in the States, and her husband felt it would be safe for her to come to the Philippines. Now he had joined the American troops and was somewhere in the field. The trauma of all the events leading to Manila's fall into Japanese hands and the subsequent internment had tipped the scales. She was rapidly losing contact with reality.

I located Dr. Hugh Robinson, a physician who had been caught in Manila on his way to the States from China. He gave me some phenobarbital to give her. I medicated her and asked her roommates to send someone to find me if she did not settle down. When I came back a short time later to check on her, she was completely out of touch. All the other women in the room begged me to remove her; they were afraid of her. There just wasn't a place to take her where she would be safe, so I approached the first Japanese officer I could find, who looked as though he had some authority and perhaps could speak some English. I told him that this lady needed to be sent to a hospital for psychiatric care, and if she were left in the camp she might harm herself and others. To my surprise he responded and within the hour escorted her out of the camp to Manila's psychiatric hospital.

It wasn't long before people began to pass out in the halls and go into shock after eating unrefrigerated food with dirty utensils. Sanitary conditions were terrible. There was no place to wash our eating utensils or to store food. Insects, both the flying kind and the crawly ones, were everywhere.

We needed a hospital with a clinic. I scoured the campus, looking for a building big enough for a hospital, a place that the Japanese might think was unusable to house internees. I found the engineering building, which appeared to be unusable because it was full of heavy machinery. I gathered the group of young men who had helped with the six rooms we previously had been chased out of and set them to work. We removed as much of the equipment as we could and covered what could not be moved. We had yet to develop an organized medical group, but we were forming a nucleus of volunteer doctors and nurses. We decided that we could make a women's ward in one wing and a men's ward in the other wing. There was space in each wing for about thirty beds. There was a room between the two wings large enough for a clinic, and there was a laboratory with one working Bunsen burner. (At that time this Bunsen burner was the only place in the camp that could be used to cook food.) The storage area in the rear of the building had a small room that could be used for two cots. The nurse who was helping me and I decided that this would be an ideal place for us. We asked permission to live at the hospital so we could be available whenever needed, night or day. Much to our surprise, permission was granted.

One of our helpers was Smiley. He was known as a playboy, but he turned out to be a very good and reliable worker. When we discussed the need to prepare meals for the patients, he volunteered to cook. We had no idea how we were going to provide food to cook, but all our plans seemed to be coming along well, and we were feeling very positive about being ready to open in a few days. As we were congratulating each other we heard a group of Japanese officers approach. They didn't have to tell me what they wanted. We had seen that look in their eyes before. So I went out to meet them and, after bowing respectfully, I told them that they should not enter because we had very contagious patients in the hospital and I was sure they did not want to expose themselves. They turned on their heels and left without further comment. Having spent most of my life in the Orient, I knew that words or actions that caused an Oriental to "lose face" would only cause trouble. I was hoping to make them think that I was more concerned about their well-being than ours. I also knew that the Japanese had a fear of venereal disease.

The next morning we wasted no time getting the hospital open. By evening every bed was filled. The clinic was opened and Drs. Robinson, Frank Whitacre, and Charles Leach were all busy seeing patients. We were learning how to make do with very few supplies. We did keep records, which we had simplified so that we could use as little paper as possible. We had no laboratory facilities or X-ray equipment and very few medications, so we really didn't need much space to record the treatment.

By this time the internee committee had organized the camp. Rules and regulations were written, and everybody was ordered to commit to one of the listed jobs. It was interesting to see bank executives and other local government employees hauling garbage or mopping the floors. A room monitor was named in each room, and it was his or her job to keep peace and order in the dormitories, as well as to assign room members tasks such as the daily sweeping and floor mopping. Space was the big issue; many a fight broke out because someone had invaded someone else's space. Several men were assigned to maintenance. One of the first things they tackled was the installation of a pipe with four shower heads in each of the public restrooms. There were no stalls, so we had to get used to showering with several other women. We were just glad to have a shower, even though we never did have hot water. This arrangement was far better than one hundred or more women trying to bathe in one wash basin. There were only two wash basins and four toilet stalls in each bathroom. Because so many were suffering from diarrhea, toilets became very important.

Standing in line became a way of life. At first there was no toilet paper, but later a limited supply appeared. One of the jokes was that each female got four sheets a day, but the men were only allowed two.

During the first few weeks of camp life, the Japanese made no effort to provide meals of any kind. The only way we could get food, once the supply we brought in with us was depleted, was to depend on the Filipinos who tried to help by throwing food over the wall. Our houseboy, Hilario, came to the wall as often as he could and held up a big sign on a stick with DAVIS printed in big letters, so that we could find him in the crowd. We couldn't see over the wall. Hilario couldn't give us much, but he did the best he could. After a few weeks, the Japanese established a package line and shed where the "outsiders" could bring packages to their former employers or to relatives and friends. This shed was carefully guarded and each package inspected before being released to the internee.

These privileges came and went as conditions changed, but Hilario managed to get into our apartment in the dark of night and remove some of our belongings. Mother had hoped she would be able to retrieve some of her silver, linens, and other valuables, but Hilario ignored the trunks with the "nice" things for the more practical items of clothing. We had to laugh when my riding boots and clothes appeared. However, I was happy to have them since they had been such an important part of my life. As a matter of fact, I still have them, and furthermore can still wear them! He also managed to get Mother's old Singer sewing machine out, which he hid under his shanty until he thought it safe to bring it to the camp. Mother was delighted and put it to good use immediately, mending clothes and making things over into more usable garments.

Everyday more people were being brought into the camp. They were brought in from the "hills," other islands, and remote places. Many were sick with malaria, dengue fever, gastroenteritis, asthma, and other problems. We were busy night and day. Body lice were invading the men's dormitories, and one day a young man who was covered with a very generous amount of thick hair over his entire body came in badly infected. We decided that the only way we could get rid of the body lice was to shave him from head to toe, then put him in the shower and disinfect him. I was amused by his description of his treatment. He said, "Six razor blades and four hours later, I was free of my unwelcome guests." Bedbugs, mosquitoes, and other crawly things were a constant problem. Little by little everybody managed to get a mosquito net, and we all filled small cans with oil or anything else we could find. We placed each cot leg in a filled can to keep the crawly things out of our beds. We also fought bedbugs on a daily basis.

One morning Smiley did not get up at six as he usually did to start preparing for breakfast. I finally went to his cot, opened the mosquito net, and asked him to get up. He moaned and groaned, turning his back on me and saying he just couldn't get up. I asked him if he were sick and did he need to see one of the doctors. He finally said no, but he had the lice and was too miserable and embarrassed to get up and do something about it. I finally cajoled him into getting up. The orderlies quickly treated him, and breakfast was served on time!

The only bathroom in the hospital building had to be shared by both women and men. The one toilet was enclosed in a stall, but since 80 to 90 percent of the patients were suffering with severe gastroenteritis, we had a problem. We did not have any bedpans, so patients had to walk down the hall to the bathroom and stand in line for the toilet. The patients were collapsing before they could get back to bed, as well as soiling themselves and vomiting. One of our volunteer orderlies, a very proper Englishman, would go into the bathroom and pick the patient up in his arms and carry him or her back to bed. He never expressed embarrassment or any sign that the job was distasteful. One evening, when things were quiet for a change, the hospital staff decided to have an awards ceremony for those who had provided services above the call of duty. We made some paper medals and awarded them with mock pomp and ceremony. Our Englishman got the top award.

One evening, about 7 PM, as I was working in the women's and children's ward, the light fixtures suddenly began to sway violently. Some of the cots moved, and we all felt shaken. Our building appeared to have no structural damage, but we soon began to get reports from the main building saying that a few cracks were noticed and there was some damage to the cupola. No injuries were sustained. We had experienced an earthquake.

Once, I awakened to find both ankles red, swollen, and painful, and I was running a fever. I consulted Dr. Robinson, who diagnosed me as having a relapse of the rheumatic fever I had contracted in nursing school. He heard a loud heart murmur and immediately set out to get permission from the Japanese doctors for my transfer to a local hospital for tests. I was sent to what had been an American hospital, where two American nurses had been permitted to stay and work. It very pleasant. I had a private room, and the food was much better than camp food. As it turned out, they could not do a blood culture to rule out bacterial endocarditis, but I did get some rest and felt better. In about a week I was transferred back to camp. I felt that I was ready to go back to work, but Dr. Robinson refused to let me. Although I wept and pleaded with him, he was adamant. He resorted to trying to frighten me, saying that I would never be able to have children if I didn't heed him. Although I knew that I couldn't even think about a family until the war was over, I did want to have children some day.

When I returned to Santo Tomas, I found that a kitchen had been established. Two meals a day would be provided—breakfast and supper. The morning meal was always a gruel, a watery porridge, made of rice or wheat. Every day, it took fifty or so women four hours each to clean the rice or grain by removing the webs, worms, and weevils. Everyone in camp was supposed to have a job unless they were sick in bed. Since Dr. Robinson would not let me work in the hospital, I found myself seated at one of the long tables in the mess tent picking the nasty things out of the grain or rice. Each of us provided our own tin eating plate for the job. I

STO. TOMAS

INTERNMENT CAMP
SCHOOL OF HUMAN RELATIONS
APRIL 1942

INTERNED...............
WEIGHT 122 lbs.
RELEASED...............
WEIGHT 108 lbs.
OCCUPATION IN CAMP
.....Nurse.....

This certifies that Dorothy S. Davis rm 25
HAS STRUGGLED THRU THE FIRST 100 DAYS OF INTERNEESHIP
AND HAS COMPLETED COURSES IN THE FOLLOWING SUBJECTS

KNOW YE.........

The board of regents, Sto. Tomas School of Human Relations, authorizes the graduate whose name is hereby affixed to exhibit this diploma in solemn proof of any stories he may tell in future years about his experiences. The board feels that 100 days of rumors and anti-rumors have given the student ample ability to manufacture convincing stories.

It should be noted also that internees have studied many additional courses, besides those required for graduation, including: Entomology, the science of bed bugs; structural engineering, the art of sleeping on a cot; chemistry and how to wash clothes; philosophy, or waiting in line; industrial engineering, opening a can, and physical education, or the missing drink.

This diploma may be used for entrance into any post graduate school for stevedoring, ditch digging or weed pulling. The board knows that in those fields particularly its alumni will justly honor their alma mater.

Sic Starvio Internitis!

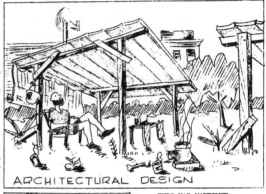

ARCHITECTURAL DESIGN

CHILD PSYCHOLOGY

THIS HAS HAPPENED

January
4 – First internees reach Sto. Tomas.
6 – First meal in old restaurant.
19 – Room monitors elected; library established.
24 – First issue of INTERNEWS.
26 – Executive committee, Earl Carroll, general chairman, formed from former central committee.
27 – Blackouts begin.
29 – First internee floor show.
31 – Central kitchen opens.
(Continued in Section 2)

WHAT! ONLY 4 SHEETS?

Humor was a staple of camraderie and survival in the camp at Santo Tomas. This diploma was conferred on the author by her fellow internees after her first one hundred days in the camp, 10 April 1942.

(Facing page) Characterization of early life in the camp at Santo Tomas.

joined the women who would gather around the tables in the eating area every morning to sort through the wheat.

Early in our internment, certain entrepreneurs managed to get coconuts into camp, from which they extracted the milk and also sold coarse native sugar. Those who had the money found that these additions to the morning mush were quite pleasant; however, I was able to purchase the milk and sugar only once.

I hated not being permitted to work in the hospital that I had worked so hard to establish, but all the doctors agreed that I should not work. It wasn't very long before Dr. Robinson put me back in the hospital as a patient, since I continued to have an elevated temperature. I was also experiencing abdominal pain. Most of us were suffering from bouts of diarrhea, and I had attributed the pain to this common malady. When the pain did not get better, the doctors decided that I might have appendicitis, so they requested that once again I be admitted to a hospital in the city. Before anyone could be released to a hospital in Manila, the Japanese doctor had to examine the patient and concur with the diagnosis. In due time arrangements were made and I was admitted to the Philippine General Hospital. I was surprised to find that I was admitted to a general surgery ward. My roommates were all Filipino citizens and, as was the custom in the Philippines, the entire family hovered over them and took care of their personal needs. None spoke to me. The English language is spoken in Manila for the most part, but the other patients in my ward spoke only Tagalog, or at least pretended that they could not speak English, since the Japanese were always watching and punishing those natives who appeared to be sympathetic with Americans and their allies. Even the nurses and doctors were careful not to appear friendly.

I don't know how the underground operated, but somehow Hilario found out that I was in the hospital and managed to get permission to visit me. He was afraid to say much, but it was great to see a friendly face. We were careful to limit our conversation to things that would not arouse the curiosity of the Japanese guards who might have been within hearing range.

The next morning I was taken to surgery. No pre-op sedation was given, and I soon learned that the surgery would be performed under local anesthesia. I must say that I was anxious, but there didn't seem to be anything I could do about it. The area over the incision site was injected with novocaine and the incision was made. I was totally aware of everything that was happening and, once my abdomen was open, I could feel everything. Fortunately, the Filipino surgeon worked quickly and finished in about fifteen minutes. He told me that the appendix was scarred, evidence that it had been inflamed for some time. When it was examined by the laboratory, it was found to be full of entamoeba histolytica, which causes amebic dysentery.

That afternoon another internee was admitted for oral surgery. She was in the next room and I could not see her, but when she came back to the room after surgery, I could hear her gagging and gasping for breath. None of the nurses seemed to be aware of what was going on, so I got myself out of bed, although I didn't think I could do it without help. Once I got into a sitting position I had no trouble getting out of bed and walking to the next room, where I found the woman blue in the face and gagging. She was still too sedated to turn herself over. I could tell by the smell of her breath that she had been given open mask drop ether, which is very nauseating. I got her over on her side and cleaned out her mouth and throat. She was soon breathing normally and her color returned. After I got back to bed, I found that I felt 100 percent better. The gas pains were gone, so I decided that it would not hurt me to be ambulatory, which was a good thing, because no one offered me a bedpan. (The Filipina patient in the bed next to mine had had an appendectomy seven days before and had not gotten out of bed yet.) On my fifth day I was discharged back to camp. I was really glad to be back where people would talk to me. My recovery was rapid and uneventful.

Bits and pieces of information crept into camp through the underground or by a radio that one of the internees had smuggled into camp and kept well hidden. The secret of its location never did get out. It was an important source of news from the outside world. Most of us did not want to know its whereabouts because we did not want to jeopardize the lives of the owner, or to lose what little information we were getting. Likewise, we never questioned the person who managed to deliver notes through the underground from our loved ones in the military POW camps. I didn't get many. Two came from Don, my fiancé, and two from Roy Bodine, my riding and tennis friend, who had helped me that last night at Sternberg Hospital. One note from Roy asked me to send him medication if I could, and another from him let me know that he had received the medication. The notes from Don were written on scraps of dirty paper. They were short, but at least I knew he was thinking of me and missing me. Don did not mention which camp he was in. I am sure that this was to protect the messenger in the event that the note was found. Almost every lady in the camp had a husband, boyfriend, or good friend in one of the military POW camps, and many did not know if their men were still alive.

Time marched on. Interned teachers started a school for the children, and, according to reports I have heard through the years, the children did quite well in their schooling and managed to stay at the proper grade level.

Corregidor and Bataan fell, as well as all the islands south of Luzon. After the fall of Corregidor and Bataan, all the captured army nurses were brought to Santo Tomas July 2, 1942. We now had some first-hand information about the defeat of Bataan and Corregidor. It was disheartening to hear that conditions had become so desperate, and that our troops were already suffering from hunger and poor nutrition and were exhausted and weak, even before their capture by the Japanese. The nurses were not aware of the "death march" and all the terrible conditions associated with it, since they had been held on Corregidor before being brought to Santo Tomas.

The Japanese opened Santa Catalina, the building that had been occupied by the religious order of the university. The chapel remained as it was, but the rest of the building became the hospital. It was larger than the hospital that I had opened, and now that sixty-eight nurses were available and could support a larger hospital, the army chief nurse was put in charge. Work hours were reduced to four per day, and anyone who worked in the hospital could eat the noon meal there. Although the meals were skimpy, they were a lot better than having no lunch.

After several weeks of internment, the Japanese government provided fifty cents (U.S. currency equivalent) per internee for food, water, electricity, medical supplies, and so on. One of the internees was allowed to go into the city with a Japanese guard to purchase food and supplies. I had heard soon after we were interned that a large shipment of grain destined for India had been unloaded on the docks of Manila, and that Filipinos had been found dumping the grain out of the sacks so that they could use the sacks for other purposes. The grain was retrieved and found its way into Santo Tomas and provided the breakfast gruel for the first meals served to the camp. Before that time, the only food available was that carried in by internees when the camp opened. Our next and last meal for the day was served at 4 PM. This meal varied depending on what was available in the city. It was never plentiful and always very low in protein. A garden was planted in an effort to supply some vegetables. The most successful vegetable was talinum, a green somewhat similar to spinach. It was a welcome addition, but there was never enough of it to make a great deal of difference. As I remember, the hospital benefited most. With four thousand internees in the camp, it would have taken a very large crop to feed everyone very often.

I continued to put in my four hours a day picking the webs, worms, and weevils out of the rice until Dr. Robinson grounded me again because I was constantly running a high temperature. He said that I had a double mitral heart murmur, among other problems. I was having difficulty breathing while lying flat, so my friends managed to find a bed with a back that could be elevated. I still did not see why I had to stay in the hospital and fussed constantly to anyone who would listen, begging to be released. When a young woman was admitted with severe depression, she was put next to my bed so that I could spend some time trying to help her overcome her depression. I did get her to talk to me, and I even taught her to knit. We had some cheap string that I was using to knit socks for those who needed them. She had been spending most of her waking hours picking at her fingernails, which she had managed to pick completely off. My goal was to keep her fingers busy so that she would leave her fingernails alone. I was only partially successful, but as we worked I was able to discover why she was so depressed. When the Japanese marched into Manila, the employees of the U.S. Council were put under house arrest together. There were twelve members, some male and some female. While these employees were together, my friend had become involved with one of the young men. This betrayal of her husband, a newspaper reporter who had gone to Bataan to cover the U.S. Army flight from Manila, was eating at her conscience. She just couldn't handle her guilt. She refused to eat; the doctors felt her chance for survival was slim. When the Japanese asked the doctors to submit the names of four internees whom they felt should be repatriated if possible, her name was submitted.

Just before the end of our second year of internment an announcement was made that there would be a repatriation on the *Gripsholm*, a passenger ship owned by neutral Sweden and used for repatriations during World War II. Most people listed for repatriation were on a list prepared by the Japanese and had come from China. My name was on the list of four that had been submitted by the doctors; however, the name of the patient next to me was not. We were told that she had been scratched by the Japanese, who would not consider a psychiatric patient eligible. My mother's name was included, so that she could accompany me, but my sister and father would not be permitted to go. I felt guilty at being given this chance, especially since I felt that my health had improved, but the doctors had convinced my parents that I should go.

When the order finally came for those on the list to leave, we didn't have much time to think about it. We were told to be ready at 6 AM to board a bus for the train station. We had no idea how or where we would be going once we boarded the bus. I was furious when a tall, good-looking Japanese officer escorted us to the train and told us in perfect, unaccented English that he had graduated from Princeton University.

The train ride lasted six long and hot hours. The windows were open, so we did get a breeze, but along with the breeze came soot and dust. We knew we were traveling north along the coast, so we were not surprised when we finally stopped near a bay and could see a ship anchored offshore. We were escorted by foot to the beach, where a strange-looking barge was partially pulled up. The back portion of the vessel was hinged and lay flat on the sand so that we could walk onto it. Once we were all aboard, the back was pulled up and secured. We later learned that this was a landing craft used to put soldiers ashore. It didn't take long to get to the ship, the *Teia Maru*, which was to be our home for the next six weeks.

One by one we climbed up the ladder as the ship and the barge constantly rose and fell in opposite directions. We were sorted out and directed to our sleeping areas. The older women were put in cabins of four to six occupants and the rest of us were directed to what had been the public areas, now converted to dormitories. My area had seventy-five

25

DEPARTMENT OF STATE
WASHINGTON

In reply refer to
SD

My dear Mr. Anderson:

In connection with the second exchange of nationals between the United States and the other American republics and Canada on the one hand and Japan and certain Japanese-controlled territories in the Far East on the other, the Department has been notified through official channels that Marjorie Anderson Davis and Dorothy Susie Davis

included in the passenger list of persons who embarked on the Japanese exchange vessel to proceed from the Far East to Mormugão in Portuguese India, the port of exchange. From there the persons exchanged will travel to New York on the motorship Gripsholm, which is expected to reach New York about December 2.

There is enclosed for your information a copy of a press release concerning the manner of addressing telegrams and mail to passengers returning on the Gripsholm, the payment of fares, and the deposit of funds for the minimum personal needs of the passengers.

Sincerely yours,

For the Secretary of State:

Carlton G. Blake
Acting Assistant Chief, Special Division

Enclosure:
Press release no. 405,
September 27, 1943.

Mr. Theodore Anderson,
Bank of Jamestown,
Jamestown, New York.

The Department of State's response to a letter of inquiry from the author's Uncle Ted, Theodore Anderson, 27 September 1943.

pallets on the floor. The pallets were head to head and side by side, with a narrow opening between every other row to get to the inner pallets. Each pallet was twenty-three inches wide and five feet, eight inches long. I am five feet, nine inches tall, which meant that the only position I could assume without some part of my anatomy infringing on someone else's space was flat on my back. Each woman had brought one small suitcase. All the suitcases were piled up together in the corners or wherever we could find a space against the walls. We found that the seventy-five of us would share two commodes and two wash basins in the small restroom. This was distressing, but then we learned that the fresh water for the wash basins would be turned on only for thirty minutes in the morning and thirty minutes in the evening.

We were dismayed to see four of the young ladies in our group ushered to cabins in the officers' quarters. However, that evening our dismay turned to shock when the ladies appeared in the dining room obviously washed, groomed, and well dressed. They were seated at a table of their own. Scuttlebutt was that the four had been selected for the repatriation because they had been cooperating with the Japanese. Needless to say, they did not have any friends outside of their group on board the ship.

Food on the *Teia Maru* was better than it had been in camp, and the very fact that it was different made it appealing; however, it was a long trip, and apparently the refrigeration was not adequate. When pork was served one evening, nearly everyone on board became sick. The smell of the meat had warned me not to eat it, and since my appetite was not too good anyway, I didn't find it hard to reject.

There was very little space on board to walk or engage in any activity, so it was a welcome relief when volunteers were requested to type the endless questionnaires that we all had to fill out. I could type, though poorly, a benefit of my summer in business school. I volunteered and spent a good number of hours each day at the typewriter. The forms were very lengthy, since each person had to report every street address, city, state, and country in which she or he had lived since birth. We had to give six references who could verify each item of information.

The voyage finally came to an end as we moored at a remote dock in Goa, Portuguese India. We could see the beautiful *Gripsholm* already tied up. It looked so clean. We could hardly wait for the exchange of prisoners to take place, but all the necessary arrangements had to be made before we would be free.

A good number of us stood at the railing of the *Teia Maru* as she was being securely tied to the dock. At first, all we could see were the native dock hands catching and securing the heavy ropes from the ship to the dock. The language they were using was foreign to my ears, but then we heard someone calling to us in English. A young man dressed in a khaki uniform with a War Correspondent shoulder patch was asking for Virginia, the patient who had been rejected by the Japanese for repatriation because of her psychiatric diagnosis. He was Virginia's husband and, as her name had appeared on the list of repatriates, he had assumed she would be on board and had somehow finagled his way from Australia to Goa to meet the *Teia Maru*. We had to tell him that she was not on the ship. I could see the disappointment and worry on his face as tears formed in his eyes. He was so upset that I felt compelled to go ashore to talk with him privately. I didn't know just how I was going to handle myself, but I knew I had to tell him that she still loved him. I don't remember how I managed to get permission to go ashore, but I did. Virginia had told me that her husband's name was Frank, so I spoke to him as though I had known him for a long time. I told him all that I could. He kept asking me what he could do to help Virginia. I had no idea how he would manage it, but I told him that if he could be there for her when the camp was liberated, and if he let her know that he forgave her and still loved her, I really believed she would be all right. I had the feeling, as I said goodbye, that Frank would somehow find a way to be there for Virginia when she was released.

6 | Freedom Gained

We had been docked for three days before there was any indication that the transfer between the *Gripsholm* and the *Teia Maru* would actually take place. It was hard to believe that we should be transported this far and then not make the transfer, but by this time we had learned never to expect anything until it happened. We lived on rumors, lying on our pallets telling stories about how great everything would be once we boarded the *Gripsholm*. There, we would be able to take showers, wash our clothes, and eat all we wanted.

When great loads of very nice luggage with Japanese names on the tags were piled high on the decks of the *Teia Maru*, we became more confident that progress was being made. However, we wondered why the Japanese nationals had been allowed to bring so much luggage. They had beautiful, large golf bags filled with golf clubs and much more, while we, on the other hand, were expected to carry our own meager luggage. Even though we had very little, it had been difficult to find a place for it in our dormitory.

During this period of bureaucratic delay, both Mother and I had mixed feelings. We would soon be free of our hosts of the last two years, but we worried about those we had left behind. Conditions in Santo Tomas were bad enough, but bits of information seeping into the camp through underground sources led us to believe that the military camps were much worse. Once we boarded the *Gripsholm* we would be in friendly territory—free to roam the passenger portions of the ship as we pleased, free to speak, but our concerns for Eva and Dad were always with us. We knew that any thoughts of hearing from them were just dreams and that we would have to rely on our faith in God and our country to get them through.

Several months had gone by since my last note from Don had been smuggled into Santo Tomas. Just thinking about the circumstances of his existence and survival was more than I could deal with. It was a lot easier to dream about the good times we had enjoyed and the possibilities that we would be together again. It was here that the first germs of my plan to get back to the Philippines began to materialize.

One day a total stranger, one of the twelve hundred passengers on the *Teia Maru*, approached me saying, "You look as though you lost your last friend. Lighten up." This statement startled me into realizing that it was time to start looking for some positive ways to handle the feelings of guilt that were haunting me. It just didn't seem fair that so many were still interned or in POW camps while a relative few were chosen to be free. We had been brought up to believe it was a sign of weakness to show any sign of fear or anxiety, and it shook me up to realize that a total stranger had seen pain in my face. My way of dealing with these feelings was to do all I could to become involved with the efforts to help those still held prisoner. To find a road back.

At 10 AM on the fourth day, the transfer finally took place. We walked a single line on the far side of the railroad track, and the Japanese walked on the other side. Railway cars were on the track, which kept us from seeing each other. Separate gangways (at the bow and the stern) were used. We did get glimpses of the Japanese, however, as we walked past the railroad boxcars. They were all well dressed and appeared to be well nourished. We couldn't help but wonder how they would fare out on the

Teia Maru. If there were as many of them as of us, and as I understood exchanges this should have been true, we knew they would be very cramped.

Before we were allowed to go up the gangway to board the *Gripsholm* we had to turn in our passports and sign a promissory note saying that we would repay the U.S. State Department $575.00. Since we did not have any money and had not been paid a penny while in camp it might as well have been five million dollars. I would not have signed the note if I could have thought of a way to refuse, but there we were, in some remote place in India without a passport. However, we forgot about the promissory note soon after we boarded the *Gripsholm* and found a magnificent feast set out on the deck. Most of us had forgotten that this much food, in such variety, even existed. Murmurs echoed through the long line of ex-internees as this display came into view. Many eyes filled with tears. I wondered how many of those tears were for those who had been left behind.

The ship was beautiful and clean. There were large public rooms with comfortable and attractive furniture, and beds, not pallets. We were efficiently directed to our assigned cabins. As we boarded the ship, each of us had been handed a bottle of vitamins to help treat the malnutrition we had experienced during the last couple of years.

My mother and I were to be together with two other ladies. Our cabin was in the bowels of the ship, in what would have been called fourth class during peace time. We were not a bit disappointed. We each had a comfortable bunk, and there was a sink in the cabin with water available twenty-four hours a day. The toilets and showers were not far from the cabin. A laundry room also was available. But best of all, we were given our table assignments in the dining room, where three wonderful meals would be served every day. We could even ask for seconds if we wanted. Most of us were unable to finish even one serving, but I did often ask for seconds on ice cream. I ate it slowly, savoring every mouthful, but also thinking of Dad and Eva and wishing that I could share it with them.

We really did feel liberated! We were free to wander the ship and enjoy feeling pampered. The Red Cross was there with winter coats and clothing, since we would soon be entering a colder climate. I did not draw any of the winter clothes because I had my old camel hair coat and one winter dress that Hilario had managed to salvage from our apartment. I felt that I was well off compared to many of the other passengers.

Surprisingly, one of the Red Cross nurses on board had been my schoolmate at Columbia University—Presbyterian Hospital School of Nursing. She was busy most of the voyage, but I did have a chance to talk to her and get caught up with news from our alma mater.

Our first stop was Port Elizabeth, South Africa, where we were taken on a sightseeing tour by bus. We saw the city as well as some of the rural areas.

Chances of meeting a classmate from New York City on a journey so far from anywhere seemed very remote, yet I had seen one on the *Gripsholm*. It was hard to believe that I would meet another friend so far from the United States. However, when we docked in Rio de Janeiro, another classmate, who had been a casual friend during nursing school, was among those on the dock, as was a family friend from Shanghai. The two did not know each other, but each had seen my name on the passenger list and took the time to come down to the ship to welcome me. What a small world!

Elliott Hazzard, one of those to meet us, was the oldest son of my parents' best friends in Shanghai, and the older brother of Michael, who proposed to me when he was seven and I was nine. The ship would be docked overnight, so Elliott invited me to join him for dinner and dancing at one of the nicest nightclubs in Rio. I could almost imagine myself back in Manila enjoying a night out with Don. I wished that he was enjoying the meal and entertainment with me. It had been over five years since I had last seen Elliott, and he now seemed much closer to my age than he had then. Elliott was several years older than I, which made no difference now, but as we grew up he had ignored me because I was much too young to be seen with an older man. We had both matured a great deal and enjoyed reminiscing about our childhood and family connections. He was a sympathetic and good listener. As I remember, many of the tables at the nightclub were occupied by passengers from the *Gripsholm*. When the soloist was told that passengers from the *Gripsholm* were in the audience, she sang *God Bless America*. She sang it beautifully. I was embarrassed to find tears running down my cheeks, but as I glanced around to see if anyone had noticed I found that I was not the only one wiping away the tears. I don't think there was a dry eye in the audience. I still get emotional when I hear that song.

As we continued on our journey, I saw Bing Crosby's film *White Christmas* in the ship's theater. I found myself crying again. Christmas was less than a month away, and Mother and I avoided talking about it because we knew that Eva and Dad would not be with us. The last two Christmases had been pretty bleak; there had been no celebration of any sort. We knew we would not be able to celebrate this year either, not until we could be with Eva and Dad again.

As we drew closer to New York, we began to have some anxious feelings. We didn't know what to expect or how we would manage, but somehow we knew that we would be able to adjust to whatever lay ahead. As our ship entered the harbor and we sailed past the Statue of Liberty, everyone was on deck, some openly crying. We were greeted by fire boats tooting their sirens and spraying water, as well as small vessels and tug boats blowing their whistles. It was quite a homecoming.

The boat finally docked, but no one was permitted to go ashore. Again, we had to wait a few days while everyone on board was interviewed by the FBI, army intelligence, and navy intelligence. Card tables were set up on the promenade deck. Three intelligence officers sat at each table, armed with documents containing information about each of us. We were called one by one. The interview took at least a half hour, as we were questioned about our past and plans for the future.

My interviewers were very pleasant, and I found that they had visited and talked to all of the people I had listed as references on the long and tedious forms we had filled out on the *Teia Maru.* They even knew what kind of grades I had made in school. They knew about my scouting activities and love of horses. They knew I had made a medication error as a student nurse, and that I had reported it immediately and no harm was done.

Some of the passengers were held on Ellis Island for further questioning. The four ladies who had received "special treatment" from the Japanese on the *Teia Maru* were among those held, then released in a few days, since they were not subversive, just self-serving.

On about the third day we were released to go ashore. Before I left the ship, I received a telegram from Colonel Blanchfield, the chief army nurse, saying that I had been accepted in the Army Nurse Corps prior to the fall of Manila and that I was to report to the Surgeon General's office in Washington, D.C., immediately. Mother and I found several of her brothers and sisters waiting to see us, as well as my father's brother Ted, a War Department civilian employee then working in the Pentagon in Washington.

Our relatives took us to a hotel room they had reserved for us, where we had some time to get caught up. Uncle Ted suggested that I go to Washington with him the next day. He also invited me to stay with him and Aunt Florence until my future was settled in the Army Nurse Corps. My mother went to New Jersey to stay with one of her sisters until she could find a job and get settled. Mother had not been employed for over twenty-five years. After graduating from Alfred University, she taught school and was promoted to principal when she was nineteen years old. She had told us stories about her efforts to appear older by wearing her stiff collar high enough to reach her ears and give the appearance of a very stern principal. I always laughed at her stories, since I couldn't imagine my mother as being very stern. She always expected us to obey her, but my father was the stern one.

In a very short time, Mother found a job as house mother to student nurses at the Adelphi College School of Nursing. This turned out to be a blessing in many ways. She had a comfortable apartment in the dormitory and soon bonded deeply with the students. Her relationship with the college staff and the girls got her through the next three years until Dad was able to return to America and join her.

Uncle Ted and I took the train to Washington. After I settled into their one-bedroom apartment, we contacted the Surgeon General's office and made an appointment to see Colonel Florence Blanchfield the next day. I was greeted warmly by the staff in the chief nurse's office and was told that a cable had been sent to Manila in December of 1941 advising that I had been accepted into the Army Nurse Corps. She gave me a copy of the cable and sent me to the finance office to collect my back pay.

I couldn't wait to get back into my nurse's uniform and become a part of the war effort. More than two months at sea, where I had regained strength, was enough to make me restless. While walking to the finance office, I was already thinking about how I would spend my money and wondering what my first assignment would be. There had to be a way to get back to the Philippines. When the finance office refused to acknowledge my commission because I had never taken the oath of office, my knees felt as though they would go out from under me. I was still feeling shaky as I made my way back to Colonel Blanchfield's office. She was already making arrangements for me to see someone in the Judge Advocate General's office. The colonel told me not to worry. The problem would be worked out. In the meantime, the Judge Advocate General's office made arrangements for me to be debriefed by the army intelligence office. The chief nurse wanted any information that I could give about the sixty-eight army nurses and eleven navy nurses still held in the Philippines. I had gotten the names and addresses of every army nurse, so I was able to go down the list and say something about them all.

The Surgeon General's office had no such information since the fall of the Philippines and did not even know which of the nurses had survived the battle and had been captured. I had written to each family with news about their loved one while I was on the *Gripsholm*. I just needed some stamps in order to mail the letters.

I was soon approached by the Judge Advocate General's office to be debriefed. One of the lawyers was assigned to pick me up each morning in a staff car and take me the Pentagon for these meetings. When I found I had to stand up in front of a large room filled with generals, I was scared. No one gave me a hard time, though, and I apparently managed to answer their questions to their satisfaction. I was grilled intensively regarding treatment of internees by the Japanese and about conditions in camp. They also wanted information about the military camps. I could only tell them the little I knew or had heard through the underground, which wasn't much. The meetings lasted about two hours. The lawyer assigned to me was very supportive, and he also advised me regarding what I could not tell anyone except the generals. We were behind closed doors for these meetings, and I was told that I should answer all questions honestly, but that I should not talk to the news media regarding my experiences except in a very general way.

Until my army status could be clarified, I was put on hold. No pay, no work. Just be available. This got pretty boring and created more anxiety, especially since I felt that I was a burden to my aunt and uncle. The apartment was very comfortable and very nice, but I had to sleep on a cot in a small space between the dining room and the living room. I felt that I was intruding on their privacy.

Before World War II, my uncle had been employed by Chrysler Motor Company and stationed in India. Aunt Florence was his second wife, who he had married after the death of the mother of his three children. They had lived in the Far East for many years, and Aunt Florence enjoyed the comforts available to executives of large companies in the Far East. She had been waited on hand and foot by many servants for years. Aunt Florence had lived in the Far East so long that she was unaccustomed to doing any housework, grocery shopping, or laundry. She complained constantly because she was unable to hire the help she thought she needed. She did have a woman come in once a week to clean the apartment, but she felt she should have someone every day and was indignant because she could not find anyone willing to be at her beck and call. It upset me when I had to listen to all her complaints. Her return trip to America from India had been very unpleasant since they had to take a freighter. No passenger ship would allow her to bring her dog on board as a passenger. The zig zag course taken by the freighter was slow and across heavy seas. It took 104 days, some days making no progress. I couldn't muster much sympathy for her, especially knowing how she had rejected my cousins, Uncle Ted's three children by his first marriage: Winston, who was eleven years old when his mother died; Grace Elizabeth (Betty), age ten; and Barbara (Bobbie), four years old. The family had been on their way to China when their mother died of influenza at sea. The children spent a year with us before Uncle Ted remarried and came back to get them. Bobbie was too young to be put in boarding school, but Betty and Win spent the rest of their childhood in boarding schools and summer camps. They never had a home. Bobbie came back to Shanghai to live with us while she was in high school.

One of the bright spots during this time was my invitation to have lunch with Mrs. Eleanor Roosevelt. Late one morning, I received a phone call from Mrs. Roosevelt's secretary. She told me that Mrs. Roosevelt had heard that I had not been paid and there was a discrepancy between the Finance Department's version of my status and the version of the Surgeon General. I am not sure just how she found out about this, but it seems she really kept up with all the stories regarding the war. The secretary said that Mrs. Roosevelt wanted me to have lunch with her at the White House that very day. How could I refuse! When I hung up and began to think about what I would wear to the White House, I remembered that I did not have a hat or gloves, and my one dress was not exactly what I would have approved of for the occasion in better times. I didn't worry too much about the dress, but in those days a young lady did not go anywhere without hat and gloves. In nursing school we were not permitted to leave the dormitory without a hat and gloves. My aunt was not at home, but I was desperate, so I decided that I must borrow one of her hats without asking first. I found one in her closet; her tastes and mine didn't exactly agree, but what were my alternatives? I wrote her a note telling her why I had borrowed her hat. I figured she wouldn't get too upset knowing that her hat had been to lunch at the White House with the First Lady.

I would have to ride the bus, so I left as soon as I was ready. I found the gate that I had been instructed to go to and was relieved that I was expected and allowed to enter. I was met at the door by Mrs. Roosevelt's secretary and ushered into the private dining room on the first floor, where Mrs. Roosevelt and two other staff members were waiting. Mrs. Roosevelt immediately made me feel welcome and very comfortable. She told me that she had heard of my dilemma regarding my status, and she wanted me to know that she was willing to do whatever needed to be done to help me. She wanted to hear my side of the story. I told Mrs. Roosevelt as much as I could about my problem and how anxious I was to get back to work. I wanted to be in the Army Nurse Corps, where I could be a part of the effort to help those who were still in Japanese custody. I felt that I was already a member of the team, but until my status was cleared up I could not participate. One little piece of paper prevented

Dorothy Davis taking the oath of office as she is sworn in as a second lieutenant in the Army Nurse Corps, with Colonel Florence Blanchfield, chief nurse of the Corps, witnessing, 20 January 1944.

me from reaching my goal. I was totally frustrated and felt helpless against bureaucracy. I couldn't go on much longer depending on my uncle's hospitality. I needed clothes, proper lodging, and work. Mrs. Roosevelt told me that she would prevail on the president to ask for a special act of Congress to waive the requirement for taking the oath of office. I was grateful for her concern and effort to help me, but after eagerly waiting for some kind of response for two weeks and hearing nothing, I decided that the president and Congress had far more important things to worry about.

By this time I was getting restless, so I called the dean of nursing at Presbyterian Hospital in New York and asked if I could have a temporary job while waiting for my commission. She not only told me they would be glad to have me, but offered to loan me uniforms and a room in the student dormitory. I wasted no time getting myself up to New York and accepting a job on night duty on a medical unit. We had decided that it would be less stressful at night since there was much less activity. I was very pleased with this arrangement, and it felt good to be back at work, but very few days went by that I did not receive a telephone call from

THE ROAD BACK

Second Lieutenant Dorothy Davis in her Class A uniform, after taking her oath 20 January 1944, on the grounds of Maxwell Hall, Presbyterian Hospital School of Nursing, Columbia University.

Washington during my sleep time. After two weeks, I was ordered back to Washington. When I found that nothing definite had been decided I told the powers that be that although I knew I would forfeit my military time-in grade and other benefits, I would take my back pay as a Civil Service nurse and then be properly sworn into the Army Nurse Corps. At this point all I wanted was to get into uniform and to be eligible for overseas duty and a chance to make my dreams of returning to the Philippines come true.

I took the oath of office in Colonel Blanchfield's office in the presence of the attorney who had been with me all during the waiting period. Colonel Blanchfield, chief nurse of the Army Nurse Corps, then sent me on my way to purchase uniforms. I was assigned to Walter Reed General Hospital in Washington, D.C., and lived in the nurses' quarters there. I was told that the telephone in my room would be monitored and that the Post telephone operators were instructed not to put any calls through from the media. Our armed forces had been inching their way towards the Philippines, and security was very tight. Many of these restrictions were to protect me from being harassed and also to keep information from getting to the wrong persons and possibly endangering others. These restrictions remained in place during my entire tour at Walter Reed.

As I walked to the hospital each morning I found that the enlisted men I passed saluted me as an officer. I had not been required to take basic training because I'd had so much "experience in the army." I didn't know how to salute, and I was embarrassed. I tried to imitate others, but I was self-conscious and wondered how many people knew that I really didn't know what I was doing. I did know hospital nursing routines, so I felt okay while at the hospital.

My first assignment was on an officers' surgical ward. I soon learned more about the maxim "Rank has its privileges." One of my patients was an eight-year-old boy who was very impressed by his father's rank of captain. He recovered quickly from an appendectomy, and as soon as he was allowed out of bed he got very noisy, even going into other patients' rooms and bothering them. One day he visited a general. The youngster did not know he was bothering a general, since patients didn't wear their rank on their pajamas. When the general asked the boy to be quiet and to leave his room, the young man said, "You can't tell me what to do— my dad's a captain!"

The general replied, "Oh yes I can, I'm a general." That was the end of that discussion.

About a month later I was transferred to the operating room, and I loved it. It was always busy, and I learned something new every day. Soldiers came from every battlefield for reconstructive work, as well as for surgeries that could not be performed at the station hospitals.

Throughout 1944 I received orders from time to time to TDY (temporary duty) to speak at recruiting functions. These were for two or three days at the most, and I was accompanied by "the brass" (high-ranking officers), whom I pressured regularly to send me back to the Philippines. Nurses were being sent to many areas in the Southwest Pacific, and my mission on the recruiting trips was to convince nurses that there was a great need for them. I had learned a great deal from my experiences and had felt deeply gratified by providing nursing care to the wounded and sick soldiers, so it wasn't hard for me to be enthusiastic about this service.

And I had my own dream about being in Manila for the liberation of Santo Tomas.

One day in November of that year, I was called to the chief nurse's office and handed orders to report to Camp Stoneman for deployment to the Southwest Pacific. I couldn't get to the transportation office fast enough to make travel arrangements. I was given a ticket on a Pullman train to San Francisco, where I was to report to Letterman General Hospital, a large army general hospital at the Presidio in San Francisco, about forty miles from Camp Stoneman. I would remain there until orders were cut for Camp Stoneman, which was the debarkation location for overseas.

I traveled by train to San Francisco, a five-day trip. I had an upper bunk assigned to me and a seat, but soldier's wives with small babies were crowding onto the trains trying to get to the coast to see their husbands before they left for God knows where. Civilians were discouraged from traveling by train, since large numbers of troops were being moved to the coast for deployment to the Southwest Pacific. As military personnel, we had meal tickets and could go to the dining car for three meals a day; since civilians were allowed to go to the diner only twice a day, they brought food onto the train and ate wherever they could find a place to sit. Many a mother sat on the floor with her baby in her arms. I got into a bridge game with three other officers that lasted the full five days of the trip. We took turns eating and sleeping so that the game could go on. I enjoyed the trip, but I couldn't help but feel for the young girls who were on their way to say goodbye, perhaps for the last time, to their loved ones.

7 | Return to the Southwest Pacific

I was a bit disappointed when I arrived at Letterman General Hospital and found that I would have to await further orders before continuing to Camp Stoneman. I was assigned to work in a hospital unit until the orders came. Most of the patients were soldiers who had been wounded in the Southwest Pacific and were to travel by hospital trains to hospitals closer to their homes. I enjoyed being in San Francisco but was relieved when I was able to move on to Camp Stoneman 11 December 1944. Camp Stoneman, as a port of embarkation for troops going overseas, was teaming with activity. We nurses scheduled for overseas duty attended many meetings in which we were told about military discipline and the importance of security. All of our letters would be censored, and we were never to discuss any troop movements with anyone. We also received immunization shots: yellow fever, cholera, typhoid fever, smallpox, tetanus, and diphtheria. We learned how to put on a gas mask and had to go through the gas chamber.

We went to the quartermaster to be issued overseas uniforms that had been designed for a specific area—in this case, for tropical areas that were not heavily infested with malaria mosquitoes. The material used was a light brown and white pinstriped seersucker. Our nurse's uniforms were simple wraparound dresses with short sleeves. The caps were also made of seersucker. These uniforms were supposed to be easy to care for, as they required no ironing, and were to be worn only while on duty in the hospital, so we had no opportunity to wear them at Camp Stoneman. I wondered how practical they would be in field conditions. I could almost see the wind blowing the wraparound skirts, exposing everything underneath. And I wondered if we could sit on the ground and climb into trucks comfortably. We just packed them in our cargo-hole luggage.

The weather at Camp Stoneman was cold, wet, and dreary, and our living quarters were far from the Ritz. We were housed in barracks and slept on old army cots. The rooms were so drafty that the coal-fired heating system had to work overtime to compensate for the cold wind that blew through the window frames. Certain parts of the barracks would be too hot, while others were cold and damp. Nonetheless, most of us were in good spirits, and we kept busy with the drills, formations, and classes on the agenda every day.

We had been there for two weeks when suddenly, with no warning, we were told that we had an hour to get ready to leave for the ship. All our gear had to be packed. Since we were going by ship, we didn't have to weigh everything, but each person was limited to one foot locker and a duffel bag. The foot locker would go on the ship as hole baggage, and we would not have access to it during the voyage.

It was still cold and wet when we boarded the ship. Struggling with our duffel bags, we climbed up the gangway. From the dock the ship looked familiar to me. I could tell from the logo on the smokestacks that this was an American President Line ship (formerly the Dollar Line) that I had sailed on a number of times. But once we boarded the ship, I found very little that I recognized. All the large passenger lounges had been converted to dormitories. It didn't take us long to find our cabins and get partially settled. Six of us were in one cabin, but we had seen the triple-deck, stretcherlike cots that filled the promenade deck and lounge areas where some of the troops would be and felt we were well off. As soon as we could, we went back on deck and watched as company-sized units arrived from Camp Stoneman. The men marched in formation in the rain, whereas we had been transported by bus. Finally, the gangway was removed and the ship pulled away from the dock.

It was almost dark when an announcement came over the public address system that we were to observe blackout procedures: no smoking on the decks, blackout curtains properly drawn, and no unnecessary noise. These restrictions reminded me of December 1941, when I worked at Sternberg Hospital in the dark with the sounds of war all around us. But it was different in that with portholes darkened, we were able to turn on the lights. Only when we went out on deck did we have to observe the "no lights" restrictions. The doors that opened to the decks were shrouded in two layers of black curtains, so that as the door opened light could not be seen from the outside. The only thing we could hear was the sound and vibration from the ship's engines. Each day, as we looked about us, all we could see was the gray ocean. We were traveling without convoy, and we saw no other ships during the almost three weeks at sea.

This trip in no way resembled other trips I had enjoyed. There was no entertainment, and the nurses were not encouraged, or for that matter allowed, to mix with the troops. There just wasn't room for games or other activities. A few of us found some space under the lifeboats on the boat deck where we could play cribbage. Card games were difficult because there was always a strong breeze on the deck. We spent most of our time in the cabin, where we could play cards on the bunk or just sit and talk or read. Even the dining areas were used at night to provide a place for soldiers to sleep. All usable deck space was accounted for, so there was very little space left to exercise or to move about. For the first two weeks it was too cold and rainy to spend much time on deck, but as we sailed further southwest, the weather turned warm and sunny.

Since we were traveling without escort, we traveled on a zig zag course that would hopefully avoid the submarines. Just once during the trip someone yelled, "Periscope!" I did see what looked like a periscope not far from our ship, but it must have been a U.S. vessel or a very poor shot, because nothing happened, and if there was anything near us, I didn't see it. Every evening as darkness fell the now-familiar announcement came over the PA system reminding us to extinguish all smoking material and to observe the blackout routine. Progress was slow, and the sea was rough. Without much to do, we were getting restless. Christmas came and went without anything to break the monotony. A small, weary-looking Christmas tree did appear in one of the crowded nooks, but it only reminded us of better days.

I don't remember the exact date in mid-January 1945 when we first sighted land. This was our first view of land since leaving the shores of California on 19 December 1944. We were told that we were approaching the large island of New Guinea and would spend the night anchored in Hollandia Bay, where some of the Red Cross passengers would be taken ashore in small boats. No one else would be permitted to go ashore. Our ship would sail for our final destination the next morning at 6 AM. We went to bed that night expecting to be at sea again when we woke up. However, at 6 AM we were awakened by a very loud blast that shook the ship from stem to stern. A wave of water pouring through the open porthole right above my bunk gave me an unexpected shower. Almost immediately after this rude awakening, we heard running in the corridors, and a call to battle stations sounded over the PA system. The nurses were to remain in the cabins until the damage was assessed. All became quiet after that and the ship did not appear to be sinking, so we just waited until we were given more instructions.

We had been hit by a torpedo. A little after noon, the captain ordered us to get ready to leave the ship. The vessel had been damaged but was able to proceed under its own power to the dock. All passengers, including about sixty nurses, where stranded in New Guinea until another ship became available. When that might be, no one knew.

The dock was in a remote area, and the only buildings we could see were temporary army buildings and tents. We were loaded into 2.5-ton trucks and taken to the nurses' staging camp, which was located in the jungle and surrounded by two barbed-wire fences. These fences were about eight feet apart and well lighted, making an alley all around the camp. We drove past a sentry gate guarded by MPs to the tents where we would be quartered. We found eight canvas folding cots in each tent. A pole was secured at each corner of each cot so that a mosquito net could be hung over the cot. The net remained attached at all times, but during the day we folded the net up and laid it across the top so that we could use it as a seat or place to write letters and so on. The only other furniture was a wooden crate next to each cot for personal storage. One electric light hung from the middle of the tent.

That night we were introduced to our first meal in a field hospital mess hall. As we came into the mess hall, a soldier with a bowl of atabrine and a bowl of salt tablets greeted us. We were not to eat until we had taken the atabrine and salt tablets. The salt tablet was to guard against losing too much sodium in perspiration, and the atabrine was to prevent malaria. All the soldiers in that area had a gold color to their skin, and we were told that we too would turn yellow, from taking the atabrine. The food was plentiful, however, and we spent some time visiting with the personnel assigned to the station hospital. We also were told how to wash the mess kits that had been issued at Camp Stoneman. Each mess kit was a unit of two metal plates hinged together by a long handle that folded over the plate and the knife, fork, and spoon that were kept between them. We never went anywhere without the mess kit and a large cup carried in the canteen pouch. Both were fastened to our gun belts (we did not carry a gun). After the meal, we emptied the remaining food in a bucket, then dipped the eating utensils and mess kit into a large barrel of soapy boiling water. With a small mop on a handle (like a toilet brush), we cleaned the mess kit and then rinsed everything in clear hot water.

It didn't take long for me to fall asleep that first night. I was accustomed to sleeping under a mosquito net, but the other girls felt a little strange and confined after they pulled the net down and tucked it under the army blanket that was our mattress. We had been given a mosquito bomb—an insect repellent under pressure in a container that looked like a hand grenade—to use in case a mosquito got trapped under the net. Hollandia, New Guinea, was considered a malaria-infected area; therefore, many precautions were taken.

At breakfast the next morning we were told that we could not wear the uniforms we had been issued at Camp Stoneman, since they did not meet the standards for malaria control in Hollandia. We would have to wear long-sleeved uniforms made of a heavier khaki material. Until we received the more protective uniforms, we were not to leave the compound. A 2.5-ton truck arrived a little later to transport us to the quartermaster storeroom, where we were told that no nurses uniforms were stocked. We would be issued men's pants and shirts. The smallest waist measurement they had was thirty-two inches. My waist measurement was twenty-four inches. No tailors or sewing machines were available, so we had to make the alterations as best we could. Our instructions were, "You may take in the waist, but do not shorten the crotch." The results of our efforts to fit the uniforms were not very flattering. I did manage to get Australian bush jackets issued to me instead of shirts. The jackets were not tucked into the pants and were long enough to cover the waist. We were also issued field boots; I found them very comfortable, but I couldn't imagine the effect if worn with the pinstriped uniforms. After climbing in and out of those trucks a few times, I realized that the wraparound uniforms would have been very awkward and also very revealing.

When we returned to camp, several of us walked over to the recreation tent to play some table tennis. There we found a notice on the bulletin board inviting ten nurses to sign up for dinner and dancing at a signal (communications) company camp nearby. We had no idea how long we would be in Hollandia, but we would not be put on duty, so any distraction was welcome. I signed up, and it didn't take long for the other nine slots to be filled. The notice said that transportation would be provided. We checked with the nurse in charge, who said that it was okay to go but that we must sign out and be back by 10 PM. The guards were instructed to check the sign-in list at ten and to make a tent-to-tent bed check. Any nurse not in her tent would be disciplined, and the officer who did not bring her back by 10 PM would be required to reply by endorsement to his commanding officer as well as to the nurse's commanding officer, stating the circumstances.

On the evening of the party, all ten of us were ready at five o'clock. It didn't take long to get ready because we had to wear our ill-fitting khaki "pants suits." I can't say we looked like we were going to a party. I guess it was a good thing that we couldn't get all dressed up, because our transportation turned out to be a big truck driven by a second lieutenant. We would have to climb up the bumper and over the tailgate to get in. Just as I started to climb in, the young officer took my arm and said, "I want you to ride in the cab with me." I wasn't sure that I wanted to be singled out to ride with the driver, but a firm hand helped me into the cab before I could say anything. I decided to tell the driver, who seemed to be anxious to talk, that I was engaged and that I was hoping to find my fiancé when and if we ever got to the Philippines.

The dance was held in the mess hall tent, where the tables had been pulled to the side to make room for the dance floor. The music was provided by a record player and scratchy 78 rpm records. We were not permitted to leave the tent except to go to the restroom, which turned out to be the typical field oil drums surrounded by burlap, which had been decorated with toilet paper to identify the latrine for the nurses. The company area had no female soldiers or officers, so this had been hastily prepared for the party and inspected by the commanding officer before our arrival. At 9:30 PM we were loaded into the truck and driven back to the nurses' staging area before the 10 PM curfew.

I did not consider this party a date with any one man and in fact had no idea that Jack, our driver, and I would ever meet again. Nonetheless, the next day, Jack was back at the staging area looking for me. We spent the afternoon swimming at the lake across from MacArthur's headquarters. I had a good time but did not feel that I was under any obligation to be available every day, so I accepted an invitation to have dinner with an air force group the next evening. I wasn't looking for a boyfriend, since I had never stopped thinking about and loving Don, but I saw nothing wrong in having friends. I had heard the other nurses talk about the air force food, considered better than army mess halls since they could fly fresh food into Hollandia on a daily basis from Australia. The air force even had steaks.

Just as I left the camp in an air force jeep, Jack arrived. Although I did not see him, he saw me, and he was so angry he left me a note reprimanding me for going out with someone else. I was irritated and didn't think he should take me for granted after two casual dates and told him so. I reminded him that I was engaged to Don and, until I knew if he had survived, I was not available for any more than a casual date.

Ten days after we met, Jack was shipped to Leyte. It was another week before our group was told we would be leaving on a hospital ship. The hospital ship was quite different from the troop ship. It was smaller, and all of the nurses were quartered in the sick bay, a large area with double-tiered bunks, which were very comfortable and not crowded closely together. There were no patients on board, since the hospital ship was heading for Leyte to pick up patients for evacuation. The ship traveled with full lights, which made us a bit nervous, but we were told that international law protected a hospital ship from enemy fire. I wasn't too sure that the Japanese had read that law, but we did make it safely to Tacloban, Leyte. The ship was painted white with a huge red cross all brightly lit with floodlights. I felt very vulnerable, but we saw nothing during the four- or five-day journey through calm waters. I was quite impressed with the hospital ship. It had fully equipped operating rooms and all supplies needed to support the care of patients.

As we approached the Tacloban harbor, we saw both Japanese and U.S. damaged ships and extensive damage to buildings along the shoreline. When we arrived at the hospital, I was met by the chief nurse, who said she was surely glad to see me. That young man had been driving an amphibious jeep in from his outfit every day looking for me, and she expected he would be back the next day.

That evening I tried to reach Jack by field phone. I wanted to remind him that I was still looking for Don. I had gone out with other men since my release from Santo Tomas, but the relationships, at least from my side, had been purely platonic. I always let my date know that I had been spoken for. Jack appeared to accept and respect my position, but would not go away. He was a signal officer, and one of his jobs was to install these phones. He had told me how to use the system, a process that had been completely foreign to me. He had also given me the exchange sequence for reaching his company area. Nurses were not supposed to use the phones for personal calls, but I bravely set forth to attempt the call. I cranked the handle of the field phone and managed to reach the first operator. Each exchange along the route to Jack's company was named for a holiday, in chronological order. Our exchange was Easter, and Jack's was New Year's. I got all the way to Christmas, when the Christmas operator firmly told me that personal calls were unauthorized. I was unable to let Jack know that I had arrived, but I didn't think much of it, since my mind was already dwelling more important things.

8 | Santo Tomas Liberated

The anxiety I had experienced when I thought I would not be permitted to join the nurses on alert for "parts unknown" was past. Minutes before the scheduled departure of the 49th General Hospital nurses, I had been ordered to go with them. I had survived my first airplane ride and a night trying to sleep in a tent just a quarter of a mile from the front lines on the island of Luzon, and now, after several hours of reflection and anticipation, I was growing weary and found it difficult to keep my eyes from closing. I was so lost in my thoughts that when our truck hit a shell hole I almost fell off my seat.

It took a moment to bring my mind back to the present. I had heard many stories about near-drowning victims who had seen their entire life flash by as they struggled to survive. I wondered if their visions had been as vivid as mine had been during the last few hours.

My mouth felt dry, and grit clung to my teeth. I raised my canteen to my lips and took a small sip of the foul-tasting water. The terrain had changed. The mountains were well behind us, so I was sure we must be nearing Manila. The back roads we traveled were almost deserted, but I

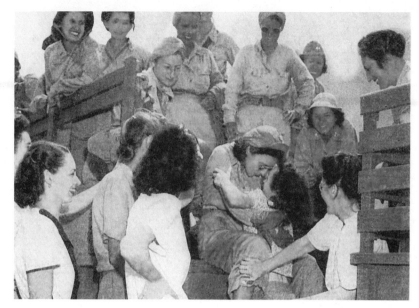

Dorothy Davis (seated, with nurses of the 49th General Hospital behind her) embraces Rita Palmer, one of the army nurses welcoming her back to Santo Tomas 9 February 1945. U.S. Air Force photograph that appeared in the 5 May 1945 Saturday Evening Post.

began to recognize the area. My heart was beating so hard I though it might burst. The fear of what I might find was almost too much for me. Oh Lord! What had gone on here? Why was it so deserted? Then I saw the entrance to Santo Tomas. The gate was knocked down, the wall badly damaged. As we drove up the driveway, I strained to see the front of the building where I had spent twenty-one months and where I somehow hoped to find my sister and father. It was partly destroyed and abandoned. My heart sank. Where was everyone?

But the area was not totally deserted. The sound of our trucks brought more people out into the open. I recognized some of them, much thinner and more bedraggled than when I had last seen them sixteen months ago. Finally, someone recognized me—but just stood there, puzzled and unbelieving until I spoke.

Others must have recognized me, too, because I heard the public address system crackle, "Mr. Davis and Eva Grace, please report to the front of the building." They were alive! They could hear! They could walk! Suddenly, Dad and Eva were in the crowd beside the truck. Their

Dorothy Davis (left) with her sister Eva, minutes after they were reunited in Santo Tomas 9 February 1945. Photograph AP/Wide World. Reprinted with permission.

First Lieutenant Dorothy Davis receiving the Bronze Star after the liberation of Santo Tomas.

expressions of amazement melted into happy tears. I do not remember how I got there, but I found myself in my father's arms.

I had returned.

We were ordered to remain in the trucks until the drivers were told where we would be quartered, so I climbed back into the truck for the short drive to Santa Catalina Hospital in Santo Tomas. The hospital chapel was being used as a press room, and as I walked through the door of the chapel, my eyes immediately found Virginia, the depressed patient who had been denied repatriation, in the arms of her husband, Frank. Frank saw me and, with his arm still around Virginia, ran to greet me. His first words were, "You told me she would be all right if I could come to her, and she is." Virginia's eyes were shining as she hugged me. I could clearly see that she was all right. I remembered how dejected Frank had been sixteen months ago to find that Virginia was not on the *Teia Maru*. The huge smile on his face now was quite a contrast. I never did hear Frank's story of how he again managed to get to the right place at the right time, but I felt that we both had a very compassionate and understanding "boss."

That night the camp came under fire again. Virginia stayed on my mind. I remembered that she had sought comfort from a young man while under house arrest at the American consulate because she was so frightened. I looked for her as the shells screamed over the building. We spent the night together, under the stairs, talking.

There was work to be done at Santo Tomas. I felt as though I had never left. Since I knew my way around, I was able to get to work quickly. The education building was to be used as a hospital and needed to be set up as quickly as possible, since, during the liberation, many of the 1st Cavalry personnel as well as a number of the internees had been wounded. The old hospital at Santa Catalina would be used as a dormitory for the nurses as soon as the education building was ready. The interned army nurses had been helping the 893d Clearing Company medical personnel and now needed to be relieved. These nurses had worked for three and a half years on starvation rations and were in no condition to go on working. I believe that only the excitement of the event kept them going. The 893rd medics were well trained to take care of battlefield causalities but had no experience in caring for women and children with medical problems. Nearly four thousand internees were suffering from severe malnutrition and medical problems. An unofficial count of 456 deaths were reported in Santo Tomas, and when Dr. Theodore Stevenson, an internee who had assumed the volunteer position of camp physician, refused to change the cause of death from "starvation" on the death certificate, the Japanese put him in solitary confinement.

Even though there was a lot of pressure to get started, the chief nurse gave me permission to visit the main building, where most of the internees were housed, to talk with my father and sister. They were anxious to hear about Mother and happy that she had found satisfying work. (At that time I didn't know that Mother was listening to the radio at Adelphi College when Arthur Feldman, the war correspondent, in a broadcast from

*Snapshots of the author's
first visit to Manila from
Santo Tomas, several weeks
after the camp was freed by
the 1st cavalry—the first time
anyone was allowed to leave
the camp. The Japanese made
sure that the city was
destroyed before the United
States troops arrived.
The author and a friend were
fired on by a Japanese sniper
hidden in the Legislative
Building (lower right), March
1945.*

THE ROAD BACK

More ruins of Manila. Below: Davis, wearing the bush jacket issued to her in Hollandia, New Guinea, is flanked by two medical officers who had asked her to join them on their first tour of what was left of Manila. Right: Filipino child (center, in uniform) who had been befriended by GIs salutes Davis and her companions.

THE ROAD BACK

the Philippines, told the story of our reunion with my father and sister.) We tried to tell each other what had occurred in our lives since Mother's and my departure on 26 September, 1943. We hadn't been talking long when the Japanese started to shell the camp again. I knew I would be needed at the hospital, so I quickly decided to return to duty.

As I said goodbye to my family, it became clear that I could not safely return to the hospital, nor could we safely transport the newly wounded from the main building to the hospital. A small aid station had been set up in the main building shortly after the 1st Cavalry arrived to rescue the internees. I found a medic and a doctor there, and we immediately set to work. We had very little to work with—a stretcher supported by two wooden horses, a few packages of sterile towels, a couple of basic instrument sets, and sponges had to do. The small office-type sterilizer was useless most of the time, since we had no electricity and the generator was very unpredictable. A Coleman lamp provided a nice white light but was not worth much as an operating room light, because it couldn't be directed into an abdominal cavity.

I don't remember how many patients we took care of that day and night. Most had abdominal wounds that required intestinal resection. I was able to provide four towels, a pair of gloves, and only basic instruments for each case. Every time another shell was fired pieces of plaster fell from the ceiling, contaminating the surgical area. We had no hospital beds in the main building, so we moved internees off their beds to provide beds for postoperative patients. The beds were in a big room, housing about thirty internees. When we needed a bed for one of the patients, we asked an internee to move out. The mattresses were soiled and we had no clean sheets, nor did we have water to wash the beds. The building was very crowded, as people had been moved in from the education building, where the hospital was to be. The evicted internees were moved into the already crowded hall. Fortunately, after about twenty-four hours there was a lull in the shelling and we were able to move the patients over to the hospital.

The following is a brief chronological account of the liberation of Santo Tomas taken from *Santo Tomas Internment Camp*, a limited private edition by Frederick H. Stevens:

Air raid signals sounded by Japanese start in September 1944. And US planes were seen by internees. Internees caught looking for the planes are punished by making them stare into the sun long periods of time. US air activity intensified near and around Manila. The following was reported on Jan 10th, 1945. Periodical bombings by heavy planes continue. Throughout the city explosions can be heard and large fires seen showing the Japanese demolition squad is busy. Camp is all agog! Internees positive that American forces have landed on Luzon!

Feb. 3, 1945—Conflagrations seen to south and east of Camp, whole sky filled with smoke. A number of American planes fly low over Camp. One pilot drops his goggles with the message: "Roll out the barrel." The great moment arrives! Supreme hope realized! First Cavalry division tanks enter Camp at 9 PM. and release internees from three-year bondage! Internees in Education Building trapped—Japanese guards on first and second floors defend building with machine guns and hand grenades, keeping more than two hundred internees penned up on the third floor.

Feb. 4—Ominous silence in Education Building. Japanese cannot be dislodged without killing internees at same time. Two meals sent to Education Building for internees. Japanese guards take most of it.

Feb. 5—Japanese guards surrender, keep arms and are escorted through US lines to Calle Lepanto and allowed to go. Education Building internees release. Entire Camp is free!

Feb. 7—All Manila is burning.

Feb. 8th—Japanese shelling Santo Tomas Internment Camp. Fifteen internees killed, over ninety wounded. The rooms on the west side of the Main Building are badly wrecked. Shell strikes Educational Building, now a hospital, several wounded, none killed.

Feb. 9th—The medical group I was with arrive by truck.

Feb. 10th—Japanese shell Santo Tomas again. Two internees killed, several wounded.

Feb. 11th—Malate and Ermita ablaze. Japanese shells still dropping in Santo Tomas.

Feb. 12th—US Army nurses, who served in Corregidor and Bataan and were later interned in Santo Tomas, are the first to leave for the United States.

Feb. 23rd—More internees leave for the United States. [Eva and Dad were in this group—I didn't have the chance to say good-bye.]

April 9—3000 internees leave for the United States.

My initial assignment at the camp hospital was to one of the female medical units. I was a little disappointed, because I had been designated with an operating room specialty. I did, however, have some interesting experiences on the female unit. Severe malnutrition with other complications was the primary diagnosis of most of my patients. I could understand the paranoia and the obsessive concern most of them were demonstrating, because I could remember the obsession for food most internees had even during the months I had been in camp. This had become much more intense as conditions worsened. We had spent hours planning meals and exchanging recipes. The internee patients found it difficult to believe that they could have all the food they wanted; several arguments broke out among the patients because they thought another patient was getting more food. One day, one of the patients counted the number of peas on her plate as well as those on the patient's plate next to her and found that the other patient had six more peas. I thought we were going to have a fight on our hands until I got more peas for the patient who had been discriminated against.

Two days after I had been assigned to the medical unit, casualties were heavy. Many patients were being brought in from outside the camp. The operating room nurses and doctors had been working for more than twenty-four hours with no relief when one of the operating room nurses came up to the nurses dorm at 10 PM looking for the chief nurse to ask for help. No one knew where to find her, so I volunteered to help. I was delighted to have the opportunity to work in the OR, and it didn't take long to find my way around, even though field conditions were far from those at Walter Reed General Hospital.

I worked steadily through the night with one of the doctors. We went from operation to operation without exchanging more than a few words.

But when I said I would have to leave at seven in the morning to report to my assigned unit, he became very agitated, demanding that I be reassigned to the OR. The operating room head nurse said she did not have the authority to do this, so the doctor stomped down to the chief nurse's office and demanded that I be transferred to the OR. The chief nurse refused to transfer me, so he went straight to the commanding officer. A short time later the chief nurse came to my unit and, with a very tight voice, told me that I was to go back to the OR. The chief nurse must have thought that I had asked the doctor to transfer me, because her anger was very apparent.

We were so busy that I did not have another opportunity to see my father and sister again before they were evacuated to Leyte, where they boarded a navy ship and sailed for the United States. The internees were being evacuated as quickly as possible, but Manila was still in Japanese hands and access to the Bay was blocked, so planes were landing on the street in front of Santo Tomas. Some internees needed medical treatment before they left. Seven young women were pregnant and too near their expected delivery date to risk the trip, so their departure was delayed.

As American troops advanced on Manila, fighting became intense and fires lit the sky. A constant line of stretchers carried the wounded into the hospital. Since all the other hospitals in the city had been damaged or were burning, only our hospital could take the wounded. We were caring for military casualties and Filipino men, women, and children who had been trapped in the walled city for a week before American troops could get to them. They were dehydrated and infected, as well as bled out, so we started IVS on everybody. In those days there were no disposable needles, nor did we have IV intracatheters. Someone had to sit by the infants' and children's stretchers and hold a needle in place until the fluids or blood had infused.

Some of the patients were infected with tetanus bacillus because the civilian population had never been immunized. All American soldiers received tetanus toxoid to immunize them against this infection, so it was very rarely seen among the U.S. troops. Our supply of antitoxin came in small doses meant only for preventive use. However, we were having to to use four to fifteen of these doses to treat each active case. It didn't take long to run out of our supply and we had to wait for a larger supply to be air dropped. One of the problems with OR nursing was that the OR nurse only saw her patient in the operating room. We were much too busy to follow up on every patient. We didn't even take time to go to the mess hall for meals. I never did hear how many of these patients died.

Fortunately, the kitchen staff made sure we got fed by bringing food to the OR. We ate in bits and pieces between cases. There was a small freezing unit in our drug refrigerator, so the kitchen staff gave us some ice cream mix, which we made into popsicles using tongue depressors for the sticks. These made a great midnight snack, as long as the generator continued running. (We were still without power.)

Once our troops succeeded in retaking Manila, the stream of casualties slowed down, but we were still busy. During the heat of the conflict only life-saving procedures had been done; now, many of these patients had to return to the OR for reconstructive surgery. We tried to get the surgeons to schedule these procedures so we would no longer have to work day and night, but the doctors were so accustomed to operating at all hours that they weren't very cooperative. One doctor was an obstetrician who was delighted to find that he could practice his specialty amid all the death and destruction of a war. He decided to induce labor on the seven patients who were now at term. Caudal anesthesia was a new development, but the obstetrician had completed a course in its administration before leaving the United States. He was very happy to have the opportunity to use his new skill. Each day he would come to the OR to schedule his induction, bragging that he would show the surgeons that scheduling could be done even for a delivery, which traditionally is never scheduled. In the course of the next week we delivered seven baby boys. All seven of the new mothers were soon ready to be evacuated together. This experience with life, instead of death, was a welcome change.

Because we were using caudal anesthesia, someone had to be by the patient's side throughout the rather lengthy labors. One of the very young enlisted corpsmen was very interested and made an excellent student. He sat with patients for hours, monitoring blood pressure, fetal heart tones, and contractions. All seven of the infants were circumcised before departure. We put the young soldier in charge of preparing for the circumcisions; he even built a circumcision board (a special board on which a newborn can be restrained without hurting the baby) and took great pride in having everything set up and ready for the doctor.

None of us had a home or family to go to after normal work days. We hadn't had a day off for months, but there was nowhere to go outside of the camp anyway. We slept, worked, and ate in the hospital, so even when we could have had some time off, we found that our work was more satisfying than just hanging around. Weeks went by before we were able to change the habits of the surgeons. They continued to show up at any time declaring that they were going to operate now. Normally, staffing for operating rooms is much heavier on the day shift, with only sufficient staff at night to handle emergencies. As things were going, we had the same number of nurses at night as we did in the day, so we were all working very long hours with no time off.

We continued to have emergencies that needed immediate surgery, but they were much fewer now than they had been. One of these emergencies was a young soldier who had driven into camp for some reason; when he entered the building to conduct his business he left his rifle in the jeep, not realizing that there were children still in the camp. A five-year-old who had never seen a jeep was fascinated and climbed into it, where he discovered a rifle. He picked the gun up to play with it, and just as the soldier returned to the jeep, the boy pulled the trigger, shooting the young man in the chest. I was in the OR when he was carried, unconscious, into one of the operating rooms. A priest in white robes was close behind. He stood by and proceeded to administer the last rites. The young soldier opened his eyes, looked at the priest, and said, "Did I die?" Army chaplains did not wear robes, and the soldier didn't know where he was. The priest was from the nearby Santo Tomas Catholic Church. The patient was clearly frightened. There was so much bleeding into the chest that the doctors did fear for his life, and we did not move him off of the operating room table for twenty-four hours, when the bleeding was finally brought under control. I sat by his side the whole time trying to keep him fighting for his life. I'm not sure of the outcome, but I do know he was doing better when he was moved to a ward.

Our only water supply was delivered to the camp in a water tank trailer. Each afternoon when we saw the men drive into camp, we would line up to fill our canteens and helmets with water. We soon got used to taking a bath, then washing our underwear in this same small amount of water. Our uniforms had to wait! Some of the men decided to dig deep holes in the ground in an effort to reach water. They did find water, but it was so muddy that all we could use it for was to flush the toilets. I tried to wash my hair and a uniform in it, but the results were far from satisfactory; I decided to use my next helmet full of water to rinse the muddy water from my hair. However, that afternoon when the water trailer arrived, it wasn't full of water. It was full of beer. The driver and his helper declared that as they drove past the San Miguel brewery, they noticed that the large vats had been hit by enemy fire and beer was gushing from the vats. They couldn't resist the temptation to salvage as much of the beer as possible. The only large container they had available was the trailer tank, which they promptly filled and then jubilantly returned to the camp. It didn't take long before everybody in camp knew that beer was available. Even though the beer was warm and the taste questionable, the novelty was enough to create a holiday spirit. I didn't hear anyone complain because they had to do without water. I don't remember just what the date was, but it must have been sometime in April or May. General MacArthur did not proclaim the end of fighting in the island of Luzon until 8 June, 1945. On 4 July, the entire Philippines was freed of the Japanese.

One day Jim Baldwin, one of my prewar Manila friends who had remained in the Philippines, came into camp. He had news about the fate of his brother, Barry, and a number of our mutual friends. Most of his news was bad, which made me very sad. I learned that most of my friends had been on one of the Japanese ships that had been bombed and strafed by the United States. The ships were not marked in any way and therefore unidentifiable by our air force. Don, my fiancé, was among those who were lost. It had been three and a half years since I had last heard from him. I had never given up hope until then that Don would survive, but now I realized that I would have to accept his death and get on with my life. At the time I had no knowledge of the number of

Japanese ships with American prisoners lost. (Don was on a ship torpedoed by a U.S. ship somewhere off the island of Panay.)

My friend Jim decided that we should take a ride through the city, which was presumably secure, to see some of the places we had known so well before the war. We both felt the urge to talk and reminisce about some of the happy days before the war. I had not been out of the camp since my reentry more than three months earlier. As we drove towards the bay area, I was shocked at the destruction. The large concrete and stone Legislative Building, as well as other government buildings, was no more than rubble. The parts that were still standing were mere shells. We soon came to the bay front, where the Manila Hotel was barely recognizable. The Army Navy Club, where we had spent so many hours dancing, was less damaged but looked very forlorn and neglected.

Just as we were about to turn back, we heard the unmistakable sound of bullets screaming over our heads. The shots were coming from within the remains of the Legislative Building, which we thought was abandoned. Jim floorboarded the jeep's accelerator, and we headed back to camp. We were told later that many Japanese soldiers were still holed up in the burnt-out buildings; all efforts to flush them out had failed. I think some of them must have died at their posts from starvation as they continued to refuse to surrender.

Nearby Bilibid Prison, where many of the American POWs had been incarcerated by the Japanese, was being used as a prison hospital for wounded Japanese prisoners. Each day a group of nurses and doctors from our medical group was sent to the prison to provide medical care. On several occasions I was one of this group. Some of our nurses thought I would take great pleasure in being able to be on the side of the U.S. Army, the captor rather than the captured, but I couldn't help but have compassion for the very young soldiers. They were lying on the very same makeshift cots that a succession of our American soldiers had lain on for three and a half years. The rooms were dark and damp. The young boys with terrible wounds submitted to our care and to the painful dressings without a cry. I couldn't help but see the pain and fear in these Japanese eyes that must have been in the eyes of our American soldiers when they were wounded and imprisoned without medical care, other than what they could administer to one another.

Once the pace slowed down, the 893d Clearing Company, the combat medical team that had accompanied the 1st Cavalry on their heroic rescue of Santo Tomas, received orders to pull out of Santo Tomas for a period of rest and relaxation. The medics left for the hills, and a full station hospital (equipped and staffed to handle the needs of the military) moved in. We missed the medics as well as the kitchen staff. The 893d medics had been great to work with. When we first arrived in Santo Tomas during the heat of the battle, they were skeptical and a little hesitant, but it didn't take them long to accept us. The cooks managed to be creative and always prepared some extra goodies. Even when the building was shaking, the baker turned out cakes and other interesting things. Although the station hospital cooks had better facilities, they never did more than open cans and heat the food. However, the boys from the 893d didn't forget us after they left. They managed to bake cakes for us while at the r & r camp and drove many miles across bumpy dirt roads in an open jeep to deliver them.

9 | The Racetrack

In May we were told that we would be moving to a race track, where we would set up a general hospital. (The track had been used for horse racing before the war but now was abandoned.) The move was delayed until the military engineers could complete the renovations needed to turn it into a hospital. It was the strangest hospital we had ever seen, and we'd seen quite a few adaptations since the war started.

We were first taken to our new nurses' quarters, ten one-story, barracks-type wood buildings. Ten nurses were assigned to each barracks with a shared area for the showers and latrines. The latrine was indeed an area rather than a room—just some burlap around four posts and no roof. The commodes were elevated on a platform so that oil drums could be placed under each seat. The sanitation detail emptied the drums as needed. Our first concern was the height of the burlap: when we were seated on the commode, anyone passing could see our heads. And it wasn't long before the small artillery spotter pilots discovered that they could fly low over overhead and get a good view of the showers.

The "mess hall" at the base of the pit area of the converted race track, June 1945.

The engineers could not obtain any roofing material, so our new quarters had roofs that were not waterproof. The first day it rained (which was the day after we arrived) we came off duty to find our cots soaking wet and the floor covered by about a half-inch of water. The engineers came and drilled holes in the floor to let the water out, but they had no solution for the leaking roof. The next morning we covered our cots with our ponchos; when we got off duty, we carefully dumped the pool of water that had collected in the middle of the poncho. This went on for several months, and we complained so much that the men in our unit decided to cover the roofs with tent canvas. This did help, but when the engineers discovered that their beautiful buildings had been defaced, they finally showed up with some roofing material.

The hospital area in the grandstand worked out quite well, but the nurses and corpsmen who worked on the regular nursing units felt that they needed to be mountain goats, because the patient's cots were at different levels. The seats had been removed from the viewing stands and the beds were placed on all levels, from the floor to the top of the stadium. The area immediately in front of the patient unit was now the

THE ROAD BACK

Looking out on the race-track hospital from the patient area, formerly the viewing stands, June 1945.

kitchen and mess hall. The roof extended over this area, but it was not protected from blowing rain. The areas beneath the stands contained the emergency room and the officers' surgical ward. The operating rooms were located on the mezzanine floor overlooking the floor below.

Most of our patients now came from outlying areas where there was still fighting. A neurosurgeon and an orthopedic surgeon had been added to our doctor's staff, so we were able to take care of patients requiring the specialists' expertise. My neurosurgical training at Walter Reed General Hospital became very helpful, since the other operating room nurses had been trained in general surgery only. Again I found myself in the middle when the doctors requested the more experienced nurses for special cases. The head nurse dealt with the problem by assigning me to the minor surgery unit, where we did such procedures as hemorrhoidectomies and hernia repairs. One afternoon, after the normally scheduled surgeries had been completed, a patient was admitted from the field with a serious head injury. The neurosurgeon was called and, since I was the "call nurse" that evening, I set up for the case. When the neurosurgeon entered the room, he looked at me and in a very sarcastic voice said, "How in the world did you manage to escape the hemorrhoid room? I have been asking for you everyday."

I continued to feel like a stranger on the OR staff. The other nurses had been together for a year before I joined them; however, they had been in a noncombat area, so their experience was limited. I was the new kid on the block.

Cleanup had started in Manila now that the city was secured, and some of the civilian hospitals were reopening. These hospitals were not equipped to perform some of the more complicated neurosurgical procedures, so the army specialist was asked to teach and demonstrate in these hospitals. He had to take all equipment and instruments that would be needed, since these special instruments would not be available at the local hospitals. The neurosurgeon requested that I be permitted to accompany him on these missions and be made responsible for packing everything that would be needed. The head nurse denied his request, so he went straight to the commanding officer and stated that he was not willing to operate in a strange setting unless I was permitted to go with him. The next day the head nurse came to me and reluctantly said, "Since you are scheduled for a day off, you may go with the doctor." She never did tell me that she had received her orders from the commanding officer. I would never have known the whole story if the neurosurgeon had not told me that he had found it necessary to skip the head nurse and go directly to the general officer.

On the last Saturday of each month we celebrated the birthdays of the nurses in our quarters by having a little party. We each received a ration of whiskey once a month, which we always saved for the party. We called it "battery acid," since it was a local product and only faintly resembled Johnnie Walker. The only way anyone could drink it was to mix it with canned grapefruit juice; I always took my grapefruit juice without the whiskey. I never drank alcoholic beverages at a party because just a few swallows made me so sleepy that I didn't enjoy myself. I could see no reason to sleep through a party, but the girls thought I was being a "goody two shoes." They said that the reason I didn't enjoy drinking was because I had never taken enough alcohol to experience the effects, and they assured me that if I drank an entire drink I would enjoy it. Finally at my birthday party, after much badgering I agreed to one drink. My friends stood over me until I drank every drop. However, they received no satisfaction, because I just lay down on my cot and went to sleep. The next morning I asked them if they had enjoyed my party, since I had slept through it. After that they gave up trying to get me to drink.

Manila continued to be "no man's land"; the damage to all the buildings, bridges, and streets was so severe and resources for repairs so limited that we continued to spend our off-duty time within the camp. I looked forward to visits from the few prewar friends who either had survived the prison camps or had stayed out of them by hiding in the hills and joining the guerrillas. One of my good friends had managed to provide information to our navy and army, which made possible many successful offensive landings on Luzon. Several officers visited me from time to time. One day a tall, red-headed officer arrived and asked to see me. I didn't recognize him, but when I read his name tag it didn't take long for me to realize that he was somehow related to Don, my fiancé. He had recently arrived on Luzon and was looking for his brother. Don had often talked about his family, who lived in Eugene, Oregon, but I had never talked to his brother or his mother and father. Don had told me that his father was a minister. When Earl, Don's brother, learned that Don had been on one of the Japanese prison ships that was torpedoed by the U.S. Navy, he wanted to see me to let me know, if I had not already heard. He also wanted to know if Don and I had had any contact during the time we were in separate camps. I told him that we had exchanged a couple of notes through the "under-ground," but I had no other information to share. Some time later I received a clipping telling of the memorial Service for Don and the other men who had died with him.

The following is copied from the press section, General Headquarters public relations office, APO 500, San Francisco:

BROADCAST 10:30 P.M. FRIDAY, SEPTEMBER 21, 1945

With the 40th INFANTRY DIVISION IN THE PHILIPPINES—The tall, veteran commander broke military custom to sing Schubert's "Ave Maria" in a memorial service held for men of the 2nd Battalion, 160th Infantry Regiment, 40th Infantry Division, who died on Panay, P.I. Major Earl Childers stood bareheaded beneath the hazy sun and sang for the men of his command who gave their lives, and for his brother, Don, a Bataan veteran, who died a Japanese prisoner. Standing in front of the straight rows of white crosses and behind the American flag which was at half mast, the commander's deep bass voice floated lazily into the still air and drifted towards the quiet Pacific and the grave of his brother. Veterans of three campaigns and new men stood side by side. Some knew the dead; some didn't. The feeling of remorse was the same for both. Occasional tears glistened on the tropic tanned faces just as they did on the new, paler faces. With stillness creeping in after the soul-stirring song, an officer stepped forward and read the names of the dead.

Their names brought to mind the death battles of May 9th and 16th, when they died. When Major Childers sang, his thoughts turned back to Bataan where his brother was killed en route to Japan, as the ship he was on was torpedoed enroute by the Allies.

It seems strange for a commander to sing for his men. But, to Major Childers, the men were his brothers. He sang for his brothers buried in the warm tropical earth of Panay. He sang for his brother buried in the deep, blue waters of the placid Pacific.

Don also loved to sing! My last memory of him was the night before Manila was bombed and we were separated forever. As we drove home that night from Lake Taal, we all sang together, with Don's strong voice leading us. I knew Don a short six months, and he asked me to marry him just a month before the war began. The song "I'll Be with You in Apple Blossom Time" was being played on the hospital P.A. system when I reported to work the next day. All day long, the words kept going through my mind. Don and I planned to be married in the spring, and I felt that the song was just for me.

One evening, as several of us nurses played cards in the mess hall, I developed a headache and sore throat. Before the game was over I had a hard chill. I didn't think much of it and slept fairly well, but by the time I scrubbed for my first case the next morning I was chilling again and felt very lightheaded. When the operation was completed, I started coughing and, wisely, one of the nurses took my temperature before letting me start on the next case. My temperature was 101.6, so the head nurse sent me to the emergency room. When the doctor saw me and checked my temperature again, it had risen to 103. Because there were no female patient units at our hospital I was sent back to Santo Tomas, where there were female units. When my jeep arrived at Santo Tomas early in June 1945 I was checked again in the admitting office; my temperature was 104. By the time I reached the ward my temperature was 105 and I could barely stand up. I was taken by stretcher to the radiology department, in what had been the education building, for chest X-rays.

I had a bad case of viral pneumonia and spent the next month in the hospital. At first I didn't pay much attention to my surroundings, but as I got better the irony of being hospitalized in the same building where I had been a prisoner of war struck me. There was a toilet and shower right on the ward. I didn't remember any room having its own shower and toilet, so I assumed that it had been added since our unit moved to the race track.

As we patients recovered, but before being discharged to duty, we were expected to help censor letters that were to be mailed. Any reference to the location or military activities had to be blacked out. It was tedious work, but it did help to pass the time.

I recovered from pneumonia and returned to duty at the race track, but I had some problems regaining my health. My resistance was low, and I became a victim of dysentery and dehydration again. In mid-October 1945, when my temperature reached 102, I was rehospitalized. By then, a small women's ward had been established at the 49th General Hospital, so I was admitted there. The doctors soon decided that I should be medical evacuated to the States. This was quite a procedure, because patients being evacuated were first sent to a common hospital, where they were held until a hospital plane could be filled. I was sent to one of the hospitals set up in the Manila area. Since I was considered contagious, I was placed in isolation for the week before a plane was ready.

Finally we were loaded four to an ambulance and taken to the airfields, where we stayed in tents for another twenty-four hours. The hospital plane arrived before daybreak, and ambulances took us to the plane. The stretchers were hooked up in three-deep tiers on each side of the plane. The floor between the two tiers of stretchers was reserved for the patients in large casts, or patients who would require intensive care during the trip. No stretchers were hung above this group. My stretcher, the one in the middle of a tier, and the bed above me were so close that I could barely raise my head enough to swallow some water.

Our first stop was Kwajalein Island, where we spent the night. Early the next morning we took off for Honolulu. In Honolulu we were taken to Tripler General Hospital and told not to leave the unit. No more than one hour's notice would be given before our next flight. As it happened, we did not leave for about five days, and then we left in the middle of the night. In those days, before jet airplanes, the flight from Honolulu to San Francisco took about ten hours. Each leg of our journey had taken close to ten hours, and we were all getting weary of our close accommodations.

When we landed in San Francisco, we thought we had arrived at our destination, but we soon found out that Letterman General Hospital was just another stop where we would wait another week until a hospital train was assembled. We were assigned to specially designed hospital cars. Patients were delivered to the army hospital nearest to their home, so all patients going to the same hospital were put in one car. My immediate family had never called New York or for that matter any city in the States our home, but Mother and Dad had rented an apartment on Long Island, New York, when Dad and Eva arrived after being liberated from Santo Tomas. They had been transported from Tacloban, Leyte, on a navy ship, courtesy of the U.S. Navy. Both Eva and Dad had gained weight and strength during the trip to the States and had arrived in New York City some time in March 1945. They took very little time off to recuperate. After being treated by the New York Public Health Service for amebic dysentery, Dad contacted the electrical supply companies he had represented while in China and the Philippines, borrowed enough money to get started again, and made plans to return to Manila. The General Electric Company asked Eva to assist them in collecting the large sum of money that Mr. Grinnell, the Far East manager located in Manila, had loaned to many fellow internees in Santo Tomas. These funds had saved many lives, but Mr. Grinnell lost his own life when he and three other Americans, the executive committee leaders who had represented the Internees, were shot. They were executed when the Japanese realized the U.S. was about to return to Manila and feared that these men would be able to testify about the treatment of internees. Eva did have reason to fear being caught with the records before the Japanese were evicted from the camp.

The trip from San Francisco to Rhoads General Hospital in Rome, New York, took almost a week, but our train accommodations were much more comfortable than the canvas stretchers on the plane. The bunks were double deck, and each bunk had a large window. The windows weren't curtained, so we had a wonderful view of the countryside as we traveled across many remote areas. The train stopped along the way in small towns and cities where one car at a time was dropped off. Chicago was the first large city; when the train pulled into the huge Chicago station, we suddenly felt very conspicuous. People hurrying past our car to their destinations would quickly realize they were passing a different type of railway car. They would stop and stare, and there was no way we could escape their curiosity. We were dressed only in army pajamas and were plainly visible through the picture window. We were relieved when the train started up again and we got out of the spotlight.

All the patients in my car were going to Rhoads General; finally we reached our destination. The railway station at Rome, New York (near Utica) was small, so it didn't take long for us to be loaded into a waiting bus. All the patients in my group were ambulatory. There was no fanfare as we got off the bus. The hospital was a group of barracks connected by long corridors. When we arrived, someone met us and said that we would have to walk to our assigned wards. Since we had been on our way for a month and had been confined to a bed or stretcher for most of that time, I felt like the distance was endless. But we all made it to the ward and were assigned beds in a twenty-bed unit.

When I arrived at Rhoads General, Mother and Dad were unable to make the trip to Rome, but Eva was able to visit me. For the time being I had to be satisfied with letters and an occasional phone call. So, I didn't have a chance to see my dad before he returned to Manila in January 1946.

I no longer had diarrhea and had received the full course of carbarsone to treat the amebic dysentery, as well as sulfa drugs to treat the bacterial dysentery, so I felt confident that I would soon be discharged to duty. Not so! I still ran a low grade fever and was told that I was not ready for discharge. I was tested for every tropical disease they could think of.

When they couldn't find any malaria in my bloodstream, they gave me adrenaline in an effort to flush the pesky parasites into the bloodstream, where they could be seen. When this failed to reveal anything they did a bone marrow biopsy and found that I was not making new blood cells normally, but no parasites. My blood tests continued to show signs of infection, but they never decided the cause. After two months, I was given a pass to go visit my mother in Long Island. We had a good visit, and I was sure when I returned to the hospital I would be discharged; but instead I was put back on bed rest (the doctors did not tell me why, because they did not feel that patients had the right to know about their medical problems or treatment). I did go before the medical board four times, and each time was told I was not ready to go back to duty. On the fourth board, I protested and even cried. Before I left the boardroom, I was told they would discharge me. I was once more assigned to Walter Reed General Hospital in Washington, D.C. I went back to work in the operating room, where I was able to further improve my skills as an operating room Nurse.

In January 1946, when Dad arrived in Manila, he found that transportation was unavailable. To get around the city to find the people who would start the rebuilding of Manila, and therefore would be in the market for electrical supplies and equipment, Dad had to have transportation. He managed to find a jeep for sale. Not a new one, but it was transportation. He was soon back in business and by July had found a house in Paranaque that he could rent. Very little had yet been done toward the restoration of buildings, bridges, and streets, and electricity and water services very undependable, but he sent for Eva and Mother.

Soon after Dad moved into the house, Jack Thompson arrived in Manila. Jack had continued to write me, and I had told him that Dad was back in the Philippines. Jack didn't waste any time finding Dad and made himself as useful as he could. He was trying to make a good impression. I had written to Jack soon after I learned of Don's death, so he felt he could now be more aggressive in courting me. He told me later that he had decided he was going to marry me after our first date in New Guinea.

Many items needed for the house were unavailable. One of these items was a refrigerator, which was necessary in the hot, humid climate, so Dad was eating most of his meals out. When Eva mentioned the need to buy a refrigerator before she departed for Manila, General Electric donated one and even had it boxed and sent to the ship for transportation. Although Mother and Eva traveled on the same ship as the refrigerator, they were not permitted to take delivery of it for six weeks, because government controls of customs had not been established. Until they had a refrigerator, my family had to go out for dinner every night. Some of the water pipes to supply the city had been restored, but they were so small that the water pressure was too low to flush a toilet or for a shower. Dad had two fifty-five-gallon tanks buried in the ground, and the city water was allowed to trickle into these drums. When water was needed in the house, one of the servants would pump it by hand into drums in the attic.

When Mother and Eva arrived, living conditions were still stark, but it didn't take my mother long to make the sparsely furnished house an attractive home. Eva started to work for the National City Bank of New York. Life was starting again.

Dad was able to sell the jeep, which he had almost ruined by driving it on the beach, where it was constantly getting stuck in the sand, and purchase an old car so that he could get around to do business. All vehicles were at such a premium that prices were high and theft was rampant. My father had never liked having a chauffeur, but he was forced into hiring one for the sole purpose of protecting the car while he was doing his business. Unless someone remained with a vehicle every minute, the owner would return to find all four wheels removed and whatever else the thief had time to take. Removing the wheels took only seconds. Since the chauffeur had little else to do as he babysat the car, he spent his time cleaning and polishing it. The old 1940 Chevy was in terrible shape mechanically, but it sure did shine.

After I was at Walter Reed for a few months, I asked again to be sent back to Manila. Most of the Southwest Pacific had been secured, and there was no fighting in Manila. My request was granted. Once my new orders were published, it didn't take long for me to be on my way. I had to go to Camp Stoneman, the same embarkation camp I had been at near San Francisco in 1943 on the way back to the Philippines after being released from Santo Tomas. This time we didn't go through all the training we had endured while the U.S. was still fighting to regain possession of the Philippines. Many of the same restrictions were still in place. and we did not know when or how we would be traveling. One day we would be told that most likely we we'd go by ship, but the next day it would be by air. Packing requirements for each mode of travel were quite different, so most of us didn't get ready until the call was made. We, a group of about thirty nurses, had been told that we would have no more than an hour to get ready once the determination was made, and that under no circumstances should we leave the camp.

Suddenly, after sitting around for several days, the call came. We would be leaving by air, and our weight limit was sixty pounds. All other baggage would be sent by ship. It didn't take me long to pack my duffel bag, so I checked around to see if anyone else needed some help. When I entered the room of Katy Allen, one of the nurses in our group, I found all her things strewn around in a completely disorganized state of chaos, but no Katy. We all started to look for Katy, and finally one of her friends came forward and said that she had gone into San Francisco to shop, and maybe she could be reached at a hotel where she planned to have lunch. We called the hotel and, miraculously, Katy was contacted, but it would take her at least an hour to drive from the city—if she could get a ride. We all got busy and stuffed her things into whatever we could find, putting the things we thought she would need right away into one duffel bag. Just as we finished packing her duffel bag, transportation to the airport arrived. We loaded all the luggage and took off without Katy. When we got to the airport we put our plane luggage on a long conveyor belt to be transported to the scales. We had finished the weighing-in process when Katy came flying in, her arms loaded with the things she had purchased and still had to pack. We hurriedly tossed the duffel bag we had packed for her onto the conveyor belt. Even before she added her new purchases, it was more than sixty pounds, so she dumped everything out and repacked. Someone found another duffel bag for her surplus items. All of the baggage that was to go by ship was put into storage for later shipment. Most of us would have been in a state of total anxiety by then, but Katy was still smiling. She had a way of getting her way and still staying out of trouble.

Soon after getting Katy checked in, our flight was called and we were sent to the briefing room. After almost an hour of instructions on how to use flotation equipment and so on, and as we were about to board the plane, another announcement came over the P.A. system: our flight had been delayed. Back to the waiting area we went. While we were waiting, Katy charmed the young soldier, our flight attendant, into putting the overweight duffel bag on the plane. All would probably have gone well if we had flown all the way to Manila on the same plane, but when we got to Honolulu, we were bumped and had to spend a few days there. Now Katy was worried. We didn't know if we would have the same flight attendant or if we would have to go through the weigh-in procedure again. As usual, we only had about an hour's notice before boarding the next plane. All our luggage had been held at the airport during our stay in Honolulu. We had only our small overnight bags with us. As soon as we got to the waiting room, Katy started searching for her friend the flight attendant. As usual her luck held out and she got her duffel bag on the plane. Our first leg of the journey was to Kwajalein, where we stopped to refuel and to eat lunch. When we got ready to board again, we were told that the plane had had some difficulty landing because of excess weight, and two soldiers would be bumped. Nurses were not bumped because there were no overnight quarters available for females. Once again, Katy had her cake and got to eat it, too.

The next day we were due to arrive in Manila. I had been corresponding with my parents, as well as with Jack, but military security prevented me from letting them know exactly when or how I would arrive. Actually, we didn't know when our plane would land. All we could do was wait and see how everything developed.

10 | Beyond Santo Tomas

I had no reason to believe that anyone would be at the Manila airport to meet me; still, I was a little disappointed. I had succumbed to a little daydreaming as we winged our way across the Pacific and had imagined a great reunion. It had been three years since I had seen Jack and over a year since my parents had returned to Manila. In his letters, Jack still held steadfast to his resolve to marry me, but we had known each other for such a short time while in Hollandia. I knew that we needed some time before making any further commitments.

The nurses in my group were taken to a reception area in Paranaque, which, I didn't realize, was a very short distance from my parents' house. As soon as we were more or less settled, I tried to phone my parents. Hilario, the same houseboy who had worked for us before the war, answered the phone. He told me that Mother and Dad had gone to see friends, the Jack Civians, to play bridge, and he did not know when they would return. I then called my Jack and found him in his quarters and free to come pick me up. His camp was some distance from Paranaque, but it didn't take him very long to arrive. Together we drove to the

Front gate of the 10th General Hospital at Fort McKinley, just outside Manila, 1947.

Civians. Jack was driving his brand-new 1947 Nash Business coupe, which had arrived in the very first shipment of new cars to arrive in Manila—just the day before my arrival. He had purchased the car for $3,500 cash (his life savings) plus his 1938 Ford sedan, which he had bought when he arrived in Manila. No cars had been manufactured during the war, so a 1947 model car was quite a novelty. None of our friends or acquaintances had even seen one. The bridge game was completely disrupted by our arrival, but we were greeted warmly, and we had a good reunion. I had to be back at the nurses' quarters by 10 PM, so we reluctantly said our goodbyes and left shortly before ten.

The next day, our group of nurses was processed and assigned to the 10th General Hospital at Fort McKinley. Fort McKinley brought back many memories. I remembered the golf games I had played with my friend Betty Bull in 1936, particularly the day that I loaned her a one-peso bill to purchase a chance on a large bag of golf clubs. I had also purchased a ticket for myself, then handed one of the tickets to Betty. She won the golf clubs! It was also at Fort McKinley that I started to date Don. I couldn't help but think about the days gone by, but now I needed to focus on the present. The war was almost over for those who had survived. It was time to start making a new life.

The main part of Manila was still in ruins. Only the streets had been cleared. Businesses were emerging in makeshift buildings, and shops were opening on the sidewalks or wherever a shop owner could find some shelter. One of the first large buildings to undergo renovation was the Manila Hotel, which had been damaged but not leveled. The Polo Club opened up in the ruins of one of the large, private homes. The Polo Club swimming pool, at the new location, was renovated and a quonset hut installed as a restaurant and bar. No polo games were held since all the horses were gone, but volleyball and softball games became popular. Life was slowly returning to the city.

The 10th General Hospital occupied tropical wooden barracks built with wide eaves to keep the rain out. The windows were not protected by glass; instead, we had nepa shutters (made from the leaves of a local tropical plant) that were hinged at the top and were lowered only during severe blowing rain. Wire mesh screens covered each opening to keep mosquitoes and other insects out. The nurses occupied quonset huts that were rather dark but quite comfortable. Each of us had a space separated by nepa screens that did not go up to the ceiling and did not obstruct ventilation. We managed to decorate our spaces to suit our individual tastes, and we were beginning to feel more like individuals than cogs in a huge machine. At last there was a life other than just working, eating, and sleeping.

There weren't too many places for a man to take a date, but Jack and I had some advantage over most of the nurses and their dates. We were always welcome at my parents' house for dinner; we also spent some time at the Polo Club, where my parents were members, or at the Army Navy Club, where Jack was a member. We managed to spend most of our free time together. The Army Navy Club had sustained less damage than most buildings and, once it was cleaned up and furnished, it was very much like the [Army and Navy] Club where I had spent so many hours before the war. But somehow it was different now, and as I would look out over the dance floor I would think of all my friends who were no longer

Second Lieutenant Jack Thompson at Lake Taal, about thirty-five miles south of Manila, 1946 or 1947.

enjoying an evening of dancing. On a few occasions I did see an old friend who had spent the war working with the guerrillas hiding in the hills of Luzon.

Jack introduced Katy, my friend who had managed to get all of her luggage on our plane after almost missing it altogether, to his roommate Bill Tripp. They were a good pair and both stayed in trouble, but always managed to come out on top. When I had to work until 7 PM, Jack would join Bill and Katy, then pick me up. One night he had enjoyed too much to drink. He didn't seem to be intoxicated, so I thought nothing of his driving us back to his camp, but when we got there he went back to his bedroom, presumably to get something. I waited in the living room for over a half hour, then went looking for him. He was fast asleep, and I could not awaken him. After several tries I gave up and called the officer of the day and asked for a ride home.

Jack's camp was quite far from Fort McKinley, and the drive was through an area that was still troubled by Huks, a native group of discontents who continued to fight the war. These men were known to be dangerous, attacking anyone who got in their way. The officer of the day was a very young lieutenant who was quite anxious about driving the open jeep through this territory in the dark. This was before seatbelts, and I slid around on that jeep seat all the way home, more frightened of the speed the lieutenant drove across the isolated and very bumpy road than I was of an encounter with the Huks.

I had left a note pinned on Jack's shirt to let him know that I was being driven home by the OD. When he awakened the next morning, I received a frantic call saying that he didn't even remember picking me up, and would I forgive him. I pretended that I was enraged and told him that I thought Bill and Katy were a bad influence, hoping that he would mend his ways. He actually did take heed and told me that the very fact that he could not remember the incident frightened him.

It wasn't long before we started to talk about marriage. We found that it wasn't easy to get married while assigned to the Southwest Pacific. The military was trying to make it difficult because so many of the men had been overseas for three or four years in isolated places under terrible conditions, with no female companionship. Now that the war was winding down and some semblance of civilization returning, they were looking for girls, and often for all the wrong reasons. The military believed they needed time to think over their actions and motives before committing themselves to a partnership that might not last when they returned home. Consequently, we had to get written permission from each of our commanding officers and be counseled by the chaplain, whom we had never met before, as he had arrived in the Philippines in February 1947. We finally got approval after six weeks and had a thick file to prove that we had complied with all the requirements.

Mother then set out to take care of all the duties of the mother of the bride. This wasn't easy in a city that had not recovered from a devastating war. There were no shops to shop in for a wedding dress, or even to purchase wedding invitations. She wrote to one of her sisters in New Jersey and asked her to shop for the dress. Of course, it took weeks for the dress to arrive, since mail was still very slow. Just days before my wedding, it finally came and, wonder of wonders, it fit me perfectly.

Our wedding was to be held at the post chapel, with the chaplain officiating. My sister was my lady-in-waiting and Bill Tripp, Jack's house mate, was best man. Jack ordered the rings through his mother, and they arrived in time, so we were almost ready. Mother made arrangements to hold the reception in the very large living room of one of our neighbors.

Dad made the arrangements for the bachelor party, which was, from what I heard, quite a gathering. The morning after the bachelor party my mother was contacted by an old friend who had arrived unexpectedly in Manila by ship and, of course, expected to be entertained. Mother was beside herself, frantically trying to decorate the chapel and take care of all the reception arrangements. She called on Jack to take the small boat out to the anchored ship and escort the friend to the house. Jack, the very hung-over son-in-law-to-be, dutifully boarded the small craft and managed to escort mother's friend ashore without losing his dignity. He even managed to show up on time for the 4 PM wedding. As Jack took my arm to walk out of the chapel, I could feel the perspiration dripping from his uniform sleeve onto my arm. I don't believe it was just the heat.

Close to one hundred friends and coworkers were to join us for the reception in our friends' large living room overlooking the bay. Everything was ready, we thought, until Hilario approached my mother to tell her that the six roast turkeys that Jack had promised would arrive from his camp had arrived but were not cooked. Fortunately, Jack was able to send his driver, Junior, back to camp with the uncooked turkeys and trade them for the cooked turkeys that should have been delivered. The guests probably never knew about the incident since, just about the time that the buffet was to be served, all the power in our section of Manila was turned off and we were in total darkness. As it happened, the president of the power company was a guest that evening, and a quick call to the power station put another section of Manila in the dark and our lights came on. (The city power company did not have generators with enough power to light the whole city yet.)

The reception was a total success, and everyone seemed to have a great time. Jack and I danced a few dances, then made our escape before the best man and his cronies could get to the car, which Jack had left guarded by Junior. Jack had booked a room at the newly renovated Manila Hotel, where we would spend the night before driving to Camp John Hay for our honeymoon. Camp John Hay at Baguio was the army r & r camp for the Southwest Pacific theater. The camp had existed before the war and had recently been cleaned and fixed up for use again. It was located in the mountains, much cooler than at sea level, and was a beautiful tranquil, place.

When the valet at the Manila Hotel opened the car door, rice spilled all over the driveway, a dead giveaway that we had just come from our wedding. We were both embarrassed and tried to appear very nonchalant but apparently did not fool anyone. While we waited for our bags, an elderly lady approached us and introduced herself as Mrs. Harrison. She told us that she was a relative of the twenty-third president of the United States and a friend of General MacArthur. After congratulating us on our marriage she told us that she took care of the general's suite while he was away, and she wanted to show us the suite as her gift to the newlyweds. We were honored, but it was hard to show our gratitude since we were anxious to be alone. Nonetheless she insisted that we spend the next hour with her. She lived alone in the hotel and spent her evenings in the lobby watching people. Frankly, I don't remember much about the suite except that is was luxuriously furnished. I hope that we showed the proper respect.

The next morning we ate a good breakfast and got an early start for the six-hour drive up the mountain. It was a beautiful drive: everything was green, and we could see terrace after terrace of rice growing. Occasionally we would drive through a small village, and finally we were into Igorot territory. The Igorots were a primitive people who lived in the hills. The men wore nothing but a G-string, and most of the small children wore nothing. If the children wore any clothes at all it was only a T-shirt, no pants. The Igorots' physique resembled that of the pygmies, small but very strong. The Igorots we saw were peaceful and hardworking; however, we were told that in the remote areas they were still hunting heads and consequently were feared by other native groups.

It was almost time for supper when we drove through the gates of Camp John Hay. Jack checked in at the billeting office and was given a key to the cabin, which we would share with a colonel and his wife.

Second Lieutenants Dorothy Davis Thompson and Jack Thompson at their wedding reception, 15 March 1947. Below: cottages at Camp John Hay, Baguio, where the author and her husband honeymooned.

Marjorie Anderson Davis and Alfred Davis, the author's parents, in 1947.

Jack (left) and Dorothy Davis (right) Thompson in April 1947, shortly after they were married, at a dinner party in the Manila home of Marjorie and Alfred Davis, whose backs are to the camera. Hilario is serving.

Apparently, the colonel had already been told that he and his wife would occupy a cabin with newlyweds. We felt a little overwhelmed, since we were both second lieutenants and couldn't help but wonder how the colonel would receive us. The colonel's wife was most gracious and did all she could to make us comfortable. The colonel had a good sense of humor and enjoyed getting little digs at us, which embarrassed his wife no end. She would flutter around trying to make amends for what she considered poor taste.

That evening, as we entered the mess hall, we ran into another second lieutenant and his second lieutenant bride—a nurse from the 10th General Hospital. They had been married in a civil ceremony the same day as our wedding. They told us about their problem: each had applied for r & r and had the proper documents for housing at Camp John Hay, but they had not thought to apply as officer and wife—in fact, had said nothing about their honeymoon. When they checked in at billeting, they each received a key, one for the bachelor officers' quarters and another for the nurses' quarters in a separate building. They wondered how we had obtained quarters together in a cabin when they couldn't even be in the same building. Jack suggested that they get their things and drive down to the village and rent a room at the small local hotel.

We ran into the other honeymooners a few times during our one-week stay. They were enjoying themselves but still grumbling about paying for a hotel room. At least they didn't have a colonel right underfoot. Actually, the colonel and his wife really didn't bother us, as we didn't spend much time in the cabin. The week went by all too quickly, and soon we were on our way back to Manila. We had been invited to use the spare bedroom at Mother and Dad's while waiting for off-post quarters We paid a little rent, chipped in on the food, and brought along Jack's houseboy/driver, Junior. I used the new Nash and Jack used an army jeep to travel to and from work. There was such a large penalty for losing a jeep by theft that each evening Jack would jockey the vehicles into the garage in such a way that both civilian cars would have to be towed away before anyone could get to the jeep. The jeep was parked facing east/west between the other cars, which were parked north/south. The garage door was also securely locked.

We had it made! I didn't have to cook, wash, or clean house, and we started to bank all of Jack's salary to provide for our relocation to the States. Junior helped with the household chores. One of these was pumping water from the tank, which was continuously filled from the city water supply, but by such a tiny trickle that it took most of the day to fill. Junior then had to pump the water from the city tank to the household tank on the roof so that we could have enough water for bathing, cleaning, and cooking.

One day Junior was too sick to work. He had diarrhea, a common ailment, but I decided to send a stool specimen to the hospital lab so that we could treat him effectively. The lab identified twenty-one different species of worms and parasites, and he was treated for them; soon he was back to work.

We were perfectly happy in the Philippines and willing to stay as long as possible. However, when Jack applied for an overseas extension, it was denied. He had been extended four times already in order to remain in the Philippines until I could get back and we could get married. I was not due for rotation to the States, since I had just returned following my medical evacuation the year before. We had been married for almost nine months when a lieutenant from personnel came to me privately and told me that he had seen orders being cut to send me to Okinawa as charge nurse of the operating room at a new hospital. I decided it was time for me to apply for discharge from the Army Nurse Corps. Marriage was allowed, but no effort was made to keep the couple together. The army made it quite clear that an officer's duty was to country only.

I had enough points to be eligible for separation regardless of marital status (all overseas personal were being considered for discharge based on points earned for overseas time and time in combat areas). I had little time to lose if I was to return with Jack as his dependent. I had to have a discharge physical, which would normally take time; however, knowing the ropes did help—I got my papers from personnel and hand-carried them through all the necessary steps and signatures from my commanding officer and discharge medical evaluation. I ended up nailing each chief of service—dental, ENT, GYN, medicine, and so on—in the mess hall and getting them to fill in the blanks. By that time they knew me pretty well, so I didn't have too much trouble convincing them that I didn't have any physical problems at the time. I failed to tell them about my past illnesses. This process could take weeks and in some cases months, particularly when they felt all past problems should be evaluated, but I had my discharge orders in hand in time to leave Manila as Jack's dependent when he got his orders.

Notes

Page 8: *coolie*—A term now considered demeaning, this was the word used prior to the Cultural Revolution to mean the lowest person on the totem pole. I have used the word as it was used then.

Page 25: *I watched the skyline disappear*—From 1945 until 1972, when President Nixon visited China, I would be one of the outsiders to which the homeland of my youth would be closed.

Page 26: *a sailor from our ship tossed a rope*—In 1986, I made a trip through the canal on a modern luxury liner and found that a man is still rowing out to the ship to catch the rope. We were told that many attempts had been made over the years to modernize this function, but a man in a rowboat was still the most reliable method. Ships are not permitted to enter a lock under their own power. A Canal Zone pilot takes over the control of all ships as they start through the canal and is in charge until the ship has passed through to the other side.

Page 49: *Philippine Scout wives*—The Philippine Scouts were a component of the U.S. Army, organized in 1901. The officers were American, the enlisted men, Filipino. Don, my fiancé, was an officer in the Philippine Scouts. They fought bravely and loyally for the United States and were the last to surrender.

Page 63: *Roy Bodine*—Roy Bodine, Dental Corps U.S. Army, was the only one of the many army officers I knew from before the war started who survived the POW camps. He had survived Cabanatuan, Bilibid Prison, and seven weeks of impossible conditions on the *Oryoko Maru,* the *Enora Maru,* and the *Brizil Maru.*

On 13 December, 1944, 1,607 U.S. soldiers sailed from Manila on the *Oryoku Maru.* Shortly after they passed Corregidor, their convoy was bombed and strafed all day by U.S. Navy carrier planes. On 15 December the unarmed ship received a direct bomb hit in the stern section, killing some two hundred American POWs. The ship began to sink, and the POWs were allowed to swim the quarter mile to shore. After a week of being crowded into a fenced single tennis court with no food of any kind, they were transported to San Fernando, Pompangua, for a few days, then on to San Fernando, La Union, on Lingyan Gulf, where they boarded the *Enora Maru.* On January 6, 1945, in the harbor of Takao, Formosa, the *Enora Maru* received a direct hit on the forward hold, killing about three hundred POWs. The *Enora* was not sunk, but it was so badly damaged that the ship could not continue to Japan. The POWs were transferred to a third ship, the *Brizil,* where they were packed in the cargo holds without food and three men shared one cup of water each day. Many died of diarrhea, dehydration, and starvation. The living shared the same cargo hold with the dead.

Since the POWs had lost all their clothes, except what they were wearing when they had to abandon the *Oryoku Maru,* they suffered from the cold. They were now in the north, and it was winter. All the clothes were stripped from the dead and worn by the living in an effort to keep warm. When they arrived in Moji, Japan, on 30 January, 1945, seven weeks after departure from Manila, 630 of the 1,607 POWs who boarded the *Oryoku Maru* left the ship for a Japanese prison camp. Conditions were somewhat better, but not good, in Japan. Then, in April, POWs were moved again. They boarded a Japanese ferry to Pusan, Korea. This was a one-day trip through calm waters. Conditions were better in Korea; Red Cross packages were being delivered, and the men were all feeling stronger. In August, American planes were flying over the camp dropping food and supplies. It wasn't long before rumors about Japan surrendering to the U.S. were heard. On 8 September, 1945, the POWs were freed. They were transported to the hospital ship Relief and to freedom. Roy was hospitalized for an extended period and then assigned to Brooke General Hospital at Fort Sam Houston. When my husband Jack and I returned to the States in 1947 we were assigned to Fort Sam Houston. We had a lot of catching up to do, but it wasn't until 1982, after Roy retired and moved to Air Force Village in San Antonio, that we were ready to fill in all the blanks and deal with the many questions I had. I wanted to know what had happened to the patients who did not go to Corregidor, or to Bataan, and why they had been—it seemed to me—abandoned. I wanted to know how Roy and the other officers that I had said good bye to on New Year's had fared. Roy was able to give me information about many of our friends. He told me that only the commanding officer knew what the plans were, and that he and the other five officers who had been left to make the final disposition of patients were just following orders.

Later, Roy had heard that the patients had been classified into two categories: (1) patients with relatively minor injuries, who could be expected to return to duty within 30 days; and (2) patients more seriously injured—amputees and so others who wouldn't be able to return to duty in a reasonable time. The first category would be taken by convoy to Bataan Field Hospital #2, and the second would be put on the *Mactan*, where, it was hoped, they could be transported to Australia.

The *Mactan* was an interisland ship that had been commandeered for the trip, which, at best, would be hazardous. The *Mactan* was painted white, with huge, illuminated red crosses, and it did safely get through to Darwin, Australia, with 224 patients (some of these patients were from Santo Scolastica, the annex to Sternberg General Hospital). The book *Mactan* tells this story: It seems that once the patients arrived at Pier 1, there was so much confusion that no one was sure if all the patients ended up on the correct ship. By the time the six officers arrived on the dock, fires in finance, communications, and quartermaster storage buildings had been started to destroy all that could not be moved, so the Japanese would not be able to use the supplies or have access to any of the files in the communications building. Within thirty minutes after the small fires had started, the flames got so hot that the two ships had to take off. The third ship, which was to take the remaining general officers and staff as well as the six medical officers to Corregidor, had to be moved to Pier 7, because the paint was already scorched by the heat of the fires. The flames, by this time, were sky high. Finally, about 2 AM the general and his staff boarded, together with the medical officers, and started for Corregidor, where they docked shortly before daylight New Year's Day.

Page 89: *repay the State Department*—Years later, in 1948, the State Department reminded me of this debt and agreed to accept ten dollars per month as a token payment by government allotment from my husband's army pay, until every cent was repaid. My husband, Jack, felt that his military career might be jeopardized if he did not meet all financial obligations, so we did not protest, but I understand that many did.

Page 106: *reply by endorsement*—A military term describing the practice of acknowledging disciplinary action by written comment to the letters of reprimand. This reply became part of one's permanent record.

Page 133: *I didn't remember any room*—In 1994 I attended a small reunion of former POWs in San Antonio, where we reminisced about the rooms we had been in. One of the ladies, who had been about eighteen years old when interned, fessed up and said that she had been in a corner room with a shower and toilet; she and her roommates had never told anyone because they were the only internees with this luxury and were afraid that if too many knew about it they might lose the privilege. We had not been permitted to visit in any room but the room to which we were assigned, so it wasn't difficult to keep their secret.

Page 145: *it fit me perfectly*—I still have the copy of the shipping manifest. Not only did the dress fit me, but it also fit our daughter Peggy forty years later. She liked the dress so much that at the age of twelve she decided she wanted to wear it for her wedding. She saved enough money to have it properly cleaned and treated, then packed for preservation so that it would be ready for her.

Page 151: *an officer's duty*—Married nurses were given very little consideration, and if one got pregnant she was automatically discharged. Many jokes were told during World War II. The saying was, "If you want to get out of the service, just have a baby."

Index

R

Red Cross, 89, 90, 104
Rhoads General Hospital, 135
Rio de Janeiro, 90
Rizal Stadium, 66 - 67
Robinson, Hugh, 71 - 72, 75, 78, 81
Rocky Mount, North Carolina, 37
Rome, New York, 135
Roosevelt, Eleanor, 95 - 96
Roosevelt, Franklin D., 41

S

Saliari, Katie, 34
San Diego, 15, 45
San Francisco, 7, 24, 99, 101, 134 - 135, 137 -
    138
San Miguel brewery, 123
Sangley Point, 54
Santa Catalina, 80, 112 - 113
Santa Catalina Hospital, 112
Santo Scolastica, 57
Santo Tomas, 2, 4, 75, 80, 88, 99, 108, 110 -
    114, 117 - 120, 122, 125, 132, 138
Santo Tomas Catholic Church, 122
Santo Tomas Internment Camp, 2,
    66 - 67, 69 - 77, 79, 81, 84 - 85, 88, 89, 93,
    113 - 114, 117 - 120, 122 - 125, 131, 135
Santo Tomas University, 66
2nd Battalion, 131
Shanghai American School (SAS), 17, 18, 23
Shanghai, 5, 7 - 9, 11, 13 - 15, 17 - 19, 21, 23 -
    25, 27, 30, 37, 44, 90, 94
Shanghai Volunteer Corps, 14, 18
Singer sewing machine, 73
Smiley, 72, 74
South Africa, 90
Southwest Pacific, 98 - 99, 101, 137, 145 - 147
"Star Spangled Banner," 63
Statue of Liberty, 27, 91
Sternberg General Hospital, 47 - 50, 56 - 57,
    61 - 62, 79, 103
Stevens, Frederick H., 117
Stevenson, Theodore, 113
Sturges Hall, 34
Sumatra, 12
Surgeon General, 92 - 93, 95

T

Tacloban, 108, 134
Tagalog, 49, 78
Teia Maru, 82, 84 - 85, 87 - 89, 91, 113
10th General Hospital, 143, 150
Thompson, Jack, 107 - 108, 136, 141 - 152,
    154 - 155
Tripler General Hospital, 134
Tripp, Bill, 144 - 146
Tropical Disease Committee, 41
Tsao Fu, 27
Twiney, 18
Twain, Mark, 7

U

U.S. Army, 23, 81, 124
U.S. Council, 81
U.S. Navy, 131
U.S. State Department, 89
U.S. War Department, 92
United States, 15, 18, 47 - 49 , 60, 66, 90

V

Vancouver, 37

W

Walter Reed General Hospital (Army
    Medical Center), 97, 119, 129,
    136 - 137
War Correspondent shoulder patch, 85
Washington, D.C., 50, 92, 97
Webster House, 27 - 28, 34
Whangpoo River, 24
Whitacre, Frank, 72
White House, 95
World War I, 17, 33
World War II, 59, 62, 75, 82, 94 - 95, 103,
    121, 124, 127, 132 - 133, 141 - 145,
    147, 153

Y

Young, Helen, 28
YWCA, 30 - 31